SpringerBriefs in Criminology

For further volumes:
http://www.springer.com/series/10159

Ellen G. Cohn • David P. Farrington
Amaia Iratzoqui

Most-Cited Scholars in Criminology and Criminal Justice, 1986–2010

Ellen G. Cohn
Florida International University
Miami, FL, USA

Amaia Iratzoqui
Florida State University
Tallahassee, FL, USA

David P. Farrington
Institute of Criminology
University of Cambridge
Cambridge, UK

ISSN 2192-8533　　　　　　ISSN 2192-8541 (electronic)
ISBN 978-3-319-01221-6　　ISBN 978-3-319-01222-3 (eBook)
DOI 10.1007/978-3-319-01222-3
Springer Cham Heidelberg New York Dordrecht London

Library of Congress Control Number: 2013944194

© Springer International Publishing Switzerland 2014
This work is subject to copyright. All rights are reserved by the Publisher, whether the whole or part of the material is concerned, specifically the rights of translation, reprinting, reuse of illustrations, recitation, broadcasting, reproduction on microfilms or in any other physical way, and transmission or information storage and retrieval, electronic adaptation, computer software, or by similar or dissimilar methodology now known or hereafter developed. Exempted from this legal reservation are brief excerpts in connection with reviews or scholarly analysis or material supplied specifically for the purpose of being entered and executed on a computer system, for exclusive use by the purchaser of the work. Duplication of this publication or parts thereof is permitted only under the provisions of the Copyright Law of the Publisher's location, in its current version, and permission for use must always be obtained from Springer. Permissions for use may be obtained through RightsLink at the Copyright Clearance Center. Violations are liable to prosecution under the respective Copyright Law.
The use of general descriptive names, registered names, trademarks, service marks, etc. in this publication does not imply, even in the absence of a specific statement, that such names are exempt from the relevant protective laws and regulations and therefore free for general use.
While the advice and information in this book are believed to be true and accurate at the date of publication, neither the authors nor the editors nor the publisher can accept any legal responsibility for any errors or omissions that may be made. The publisher makes no warranty, express or implied, with respect to the material contained herein.

Printed on acid-free paper

Springer is part of Springer Science+Business Media (www.springer.com)

About this Book

This brief examines the influence and prestige of scholars and works in the field of criminology and criminal justice, as well as changes in influence and prestige over a period of 25 years, based on citation analysis. Methods of measuring scholarly influence can be highly controversial, but the authors of this work clearly outline their methodology, developed over years of experience working in this area of study. Through their expertise in criminology and criminal justice, they are able to solve problems that affect or confound many traditional forms of citation analysis, such as irregularly cited references or self-citations. This book includes 25 years of data (1986 through 2010) on the most-cited scholars and works in major American and international criminology and criminal justice journals and provides an objective measure of influence and prestige. Through an analysis of the data, the authors also document the intellectual development of criminology and criminal justice as a field of study since 1986. They highlight the development of research trends and indicate areas for future research. This book is designed for use by scholars and academics in the fields of criminology and criminal justice, and the methodology will be of interest to researchers in related disciplines, including sociology and social psychology.

'Cohn, Farrington, and Iratzoqui provide an invaluable service in unpacking the criminological enterprise. Using systematic citational analysis, they illuminate the core patterns of scholarly influence that have shaped the field's development. This volume is an essential resource for all those wishing to understand which scholars and writings have done most—within and across time periods—to affect thinking about crime and justice'.

Francis T. Cullen
Distinguished Research Professor
University of Cincinnati

'Citation analyses have become one of the most significant measures of scholarly influence. They are especially useful for revealing major trends over time regarding authors and the topics of interest to the wider field. Cohn, Farrington, and Iratzoqui's Most Cited Scholars in Criminology and Criminal Justice, 1986–2010 provides the most up-to-date, comprehensive, and longitudinal investigation of scholarly influence in criminology/criminal justice. This resource is a very interesting read, one that supplies not a mere counting of citations but clear ideas about where the field has been centered and where it is trending into the future'.

Alex R. Piquero
Ashbel Smith Professor of Criminology
University of Texas at Dallas

Preface

This book documents the most-cited scholars in major criminology and criminal justice (CCJ) journals, and their most-cited works, over a 25-year period. It is based on the assumption that the most-cited scholars tend to be the most influential in the field. Three series of longitudinal analyses are described: (a) the most-cited scholars in 4 international journals from 1986–1990 to 2006–2010; (b) the most-cited scholars in 6 American journals from 1986–1990 to 2006–2010; and (c) the most-cited scholars in 20 American and international journals from 1990 to 2010.

We studied citations in a small number of the most prestigious CCJ journals in order to overcome the many problems (described in Chapter 1) of using large-scale sources of citations such as Web of Science, Google Scholar, and Scopus. The main strength of our research lies in its careful checking and correcting of citations, its exclusion of self-citations, and its longitudinal comparative analyses (using exactly the same methods) over a 25-year period.

Circumstances were very different when we began our research in 1988. There was no Internet and very little interest in citation analysis or any other research on scholarly influence in criminology and criminal justice. In the past 25 years, there has been a massive increase in interest in research on scholarly influence in general and citation analysis in particular. The Internet and electronic resources make large-scale citation analyses a lot easier but such analyses are typically full of problems and errors that have been corrected in our analyses.

We trace the waxing and waning of scholarly influence over time, as older scholars such as Marvin E. Wolfgang give way to younger scholars such as Robert J. Sampson, who in turn are now being usurped by still younger scholars such as Alex R. Piquero. We carried out this research without funding, because we were curious about the results. Citation research is highly controversial. While many scholars are fascinated by the results, others (especially those who are not highly cited) are very hostile to citation analysis. Nevertheless, it is clear that citation analysis is very important, and it has the advantage of being a scientific, objective, quantitative technique. The raw data (citations in journals) are freely available to anyone who wishes to replicate our analyses. However, researchers should be warned that there were over 500,000 cited authors in nine major CCJ journals during our 25-year period.

We hope that readers will find our results fascinating. We are very grateful to Maureen Brown for providing excellent secretarial assistance throughout the time period of this research.

May 2013

Miami, FL Ellen G. Cohn
Cambridge, UK David P. Farrington
Tallahassee, FL Amaia Iratzoqui

Contents

1 Citation Analysis in Criminology and Criminal Justice 1
    1.1 Overview 1
    1.2 Uses of Citation Analysis 2
    1.3 Sources of Data 3
    1.4 Cohn and Farrington's Citation Research 3
    1.5 Most-Cited Scholars and Works in Four Major
          International Journals 4
    1.6 Most-Cited Scholars and Works in Six Major
          American Journals 7
    1.7 Most-Cited Scholars and Works in 20 Journals 9
    1.8 Criminal Career Concepts in Citation Analysis 12
    1.9 Limitations of Citation Analysis 12
    1.10 Conclusion 13

2 Methodology 15
    2.1 Selecting a Source of Citation Data 15
    2.2 Journal Selection 16
    2.3 Selecting Four International Journals 17
    2.4 Selecting Six American Journals 18
    2.5 Selecting 20 American and International Journals 19
    2.6 Obtaining the Citation Data 21
    2.7 Counting Citations 22
    2.8 Limitations of This Methodology 23
    2.9 Strengths of This Methodology 24
    2.10 The Current Research 25

3 Most-Cited Scholars in Four International Journals 27
    3.1 *Australian and New Zealand Journal of Criminology* (ANZ) 27
    3.2 *British Journal of Criminology* (BJC) 28
    3.3 *Canadian Journal of Criminology and Criminal Justice* (CJC) 32

	3.4 *Criminology* (CRIM)	35
	3.5 Most-Cited Scholars in All Four Journals	37
	3.6 Conclusion	42
4	**Most-Cited Scholars in Six American Criminology and Criminal Justice Journals**	**45**
	4.1 *Journal of Quantitative Criminology* (JQC)	45
	4.2 *Journal of Research in Crime and Delinquency* (JRCD)	48
	4.3 Most-Cited Scholars in Three Criminology Journals	50
	4.4 *Justice Quarterly* (JQ)	53
	4.5 *Journal of Criminal Justice* (JCJ)	56
	4.6 *Criminal Justice and Behavior* (CJB)	58
	4.7 Most-Cited Scholars in Three Criminal Justice Journals	61
	4.8 Most-Cited Scholars in Six American Journals	64
	4.9 Conclusion	67
5	**Most-Cited Scholars in 20 Journals**	**69**
	5.1 Citations in 20 Journals	69
	5.2 Most-Cited Scholars in Each Journal	71
	5.3 Most-Cited Scholars in Five Journals	71
	5.4 Most-Cited Scholars in Ten Journals	75
	5.5 Most-Cited Scholars in 20 Journals	77
	5.6 Further Analyses	80
	5.7 Conclusion	83
6	**Conclusions**	**87**
	6.1 The Main Contribution of This Book	87
	6.2 Policy Implications	88
	6.3 Future Citation Research	90
References		**93**
About the Authors		**101**
Name Index		**103**
Subject Index		**109**

Chapter 1
Citation Analysis in Criminology and Criminal Justice

1.1 Overview

Our goal in writing *Most-Cited Scholars in Criminology and Criminal Justice, 1986–2010* is to create a text that examines the influence and prestige of scholars and works in the field of criminology and criminal justice (CCJ), as well as changes in influence and prestige over a period of 25 years, based on citation analysis. This book builds upon many years of research done by Cohn and Farrington in the field of citation analysis. The previous research has examined changes within and across specific time periods and across a wide range of major CCJ journals. Their recent book, *Scholarly Influence in Criminology and Criminal Justice* (Cohn & Farrington, 2012b), focused on citations in major journals in 2001–2005 and in previous years as well as on publication productivity.

The current work updates and expands this research by adding citations from 2006 to 2010 to examine changes over a longer time period, in groups of 4 major international CCJ journals, 6 major American CCJ journals, and 20 major international and American criminology and criminal justice journals. Our analysis covers 25 years of data (1986 through 2010) on the most-cited scholars in major journals. This chapter reviews the importance of citation research as a means of examining prestige and influence in CCJ, including studies using citation analysis to evaluate scholars, journals, published works, and university departments. More specifically, this chapter describes existing studies using the methodology developed by Cohn and Farrington and provides a sense of direction for our current research on the most-cited scholars in American and international criminology and criminology justice journals from 1986 to 2010.

1.2 Uses of Citation Analysis

Citation analysis provides an objective quantitative method for determining the impact of a scholar, journal, or department on the field (Cohn & Farrington, 2005). The main assumptions in citation analysis are that highly cited works are important to the scholars who cite them and that citations indicate scholarly influence (Meadows, 1974). Essentially, if multiple researchers working independently on the same problem all cite the same source, that material is considered to have scholarly influence. If a scholar's work is highly cited, it suggests that others in the field find that scholar's work important and valuable. Cohn and Farrington (1994a) define influential scholars as those who are most cited in the major criminological journals. Thus, scholarly influence refers not only to the actual number of citations but also to the fact that these numerous citations are in articles published by the most prestigious CCJ journals.

This method is objective and replicable. The raw citation data are readily available for scholars who wish to replicate the findings of any citation analysis. Identifying the most-cited authors in major CCJ journals helps to identify the most influential scholars and topics during a particular time period and to document the historical development of the field (Cohn & Farrington, 1998b, 2012b). For example, the recent presence of Robert J. Sampson as 1 of the top-cited scholars indicates the enduring influence of his follow-ups of the Glueck boys (Laub & Sampson, 2003; Sampson & Laub, 1993) and his work on collective efficacy (Sampson, Raudenbush, & Earls, 1997).

Citation analysis rose to prominence with Wolfgang, Figlio, and Thornberry's (1978) book *Evaluating Criminology*. They used this technique to determine the most-cited American books and journal articles in criminology between 1945 and 1972. Their work, which examined citations in almost 4,000 scholarly publications, revealed a characteristically skewed distribution. A small number of publications were highly cited, while the remainder received few or no citations. Twenty years later, their research inspired Cohn, Farrington, and Wright (1998) to return to the topic in their book, *Evaluating Criminology and Criminal Justice*. In this book, these authors used citation analysis to examine the most-cited scholars and works in a variety of American and international journals in criminology and criminal justice over a 10-year (1986–1995) period. Similar to their predecessors, Cohn and colleagues observed that, like "chronic offenders," a small number of scholars accounted for a disproportionate fraction of all citations (see also Cohn & Farrington, 1994a).

In addition to studying scholarly influence and prestige, citation analysis has also been applied to other topics, as well. Research on the quality of doctoral program faculty has been assessed by counting the number of citations of their publications (Cohn & Farrington, 1998c; DeZee, 1980; Sorenson, Patterson, & Widmayer, 1992, 1993; Thomas & Bronick, 1984). Faculty whose work is more often cited can be viewed as being more influential, which brings greater prestige to their department and their university. This perspective has been developed into a subsidiary form of citation analysis, known as productivity analysis. Productivity analysis, which looks at the productivity of faculty members in terms of their number of publications, has been used in CCJ to evaluate CCJ departments (Cohn & Farrington, 1998c; Cohn,

Farrington, & Sorenson, 2000; Davis & Sorenson, 2010; DeZee, 1980; Fabianic, 1981, 2001, 2002; Kleck & Barnes, 2011; Kleck, Wang, & Tark, 2007; Oliver, Swindell, Marks, & Balusek, 2009; Parker & Goldfeder, 1979; Sorenson, 1994; Sorenson et al., 1992; Sorenson & Pilgrim, 2002; Steiner & Schwartz, 2006, 2007; Taggart & Holmes, 1991). It has also been used either in place of or in addition to citation analysis to study the scholarly influence of individual scholars in CCJ (Cohn et al., 2000; Fabianic, 2012; Frost, Phillips, & Clear, 2007; Jennings, Gibson, Ward, & Beaver, 2008; Jennings, Schreck, Sturtz, & Mahoney, 2008; Khey, Jennings, Higgins, Schoepfer, & Langton, 2011; Long, Boggess, & Jennings, 2011; Oliver et al., 2009; Orrick & Weir, 2011; Rice, Cohn, & Farrington, 2005; Rice, Terry, Miller, & Ackerman, 2007; Shutt & Barnes, 2008; Stack, 2001; Steiner & Schwartz, 2006, 2007).

1.3 Sources of Data

There are 3 main sources of citation data in CCJ (Cohn, 2009; Cohn & Farrington, 2012b). The first is Thomson Reuters' Web of Science, which includes the Science Citation Index, the Social Sciences Citation Index (SSCI), and the Arts and Humanities Citation Index (AHCI). These indexes list literally millions of bibliographic references made in thousands of journals published throughout the world. For the purposes of criminological research, the SSCI is clearly the most useful of the three. The second source of citation data is online scientific archives, such as Elsevier's Scopus and Google Scholar, both of which have been in operation since 2004. SSCI, Scopus, and Google Scholar overlap but each source includes different citation data and, as a result, each produces different results; in general, Scopus and especially Google Scholar produce higher citation counts than SSCI. Both SSCI and the various online archives have a number of problems and limitations that may significantly impact the accuracy of any research (Cohn & Farrington, 2012b, pp. 1–21).

The third method of gathering citation data involves examining the reference lists of journals, scholarly books, textbooks, monographs, and other works in a given field and counting the number of citations of a given scholar, scholarly work, or journal. Although this method is considerably more labor intensive and time consuming, it does permit researchers to avoid many of the problems inherent in the use of SSCI and other citation indexes. The technique of studying only the most prestigious journals in CCJ was pioneered by Cohn and Farrington (1990) and is described in detail in Chapter 2.

1.4 Cohn and Farrington's Citation Research

Cohn and Farrington have been working and publishing in the area of citation analysis for over 20 years. According to Cullen (2012, p. viii), they "have been the leading scholars in the use of citations to assess scholarly influence within criminology" and are widely recognized as 2 of the leading experts in the field. One reason for this acclaim is because they try hard to minimize errors and their method of citation research is objective and easily replicable, as the data are publicly available. The major results of their research may be found in a series of books and articles published between 1990 and 2012.

There are 3 main areas of their research, all of which focus on identifying the most-cited scholars and works in criminology and criminal justice journals. The first examines the major CCJ journals in the United States and in the major English-speaking countries around the world (Australia and New Zealand, Canada, and the United Kingdom). The second focuses specifically on American CCJ journals, looking at 3 major criminology journals and 3 major criminal justice journals. Finally, their third stream of research examines 20 American and international journals, including the 9 journals studied in the first 2 research series and adding an additional 11 journals. Each of these research areas is discussed individually.

While the results of each stream of research varies by time period, as the influence of scholars and works waxes and wanes, there is a considerable amount of consistency when the results are compared within each wave. This consistency within a replicated methodology indicates a high degree of internal reliability. Additionally, the most influential scholars identified by citation analysis tend to be those identified by other measures of scholarly influence, which also demonstrates the validity of this methodology (Cohn & Farrington, 1995).

1.5 Most-Cited Scholars and Works in Four Major International Journals

Cohn and Farrington's first foray into the field of citation analysis (Cohn & Farrington, 1990) compared citations in 1 American journal (*Criminology*) and 1 British journal (the *British Journal of Criminology*). They subsequently expanded their focus to include the major CCJ journals in 3 additional English-language countries: Canada (the *Canadian Journal of Criminology*; now the *Canadian Journal of Criminology and Criminal Justice*) and Australia and New Zealand (the *Australian and New Zealand Journal of Criminology*). The goal of the research was to determine the most influential scholars in CCJ in the English-speaking world by examining all citations in these journals during the 5-year period 1986–1990 (Cohn & Farrington, 1994a).

Using a combined measure of influence that controlled for the number of citations in a journal and thus gave equal weight to citations in all 4 journals, they found that the most-cited scholars were Marvin E. Wolfgang, Alfred Blumstein, David P. Farrington, James Q. Wilson, and Stanley Cohen. They also examined the most-cited publications of these scholars and found that in most cases, their high citation counts were driven at least in part by the large number of different works that were cited. Interestingly, while they discovered that scholars who were highly cited in

Criminology tended to be highly cited in the other 3 journals as well, the reverse was not true; highly cited scholars in the non-American journals tended not to be highly cited in *Criminology*. In particular, the most highly-cited scholars in the *Australian and New Zealand Journal of Criminology* tended to be the *least* highly cited in the other 3 journals, suggesting that it was the most isolated journal. They also found that *Criminology* had the lowest proportion of nonnative highly cited scholars; the vast majority of citations in that journal were of American scholars, whereas much larger proportions of citations in the other 3 journals were of scholars in other countries. Therefore, *Criminology* was the most parochial of the 4 journals.

This line of research was continued over subsequent 5-year periods, using the same 4 journals, to assess changes in scholarly influence over time. In the second wave, which covered the years 1991–1995 (Cohn & Farrington, 1998a; see also Cohn et al., 1998), the most-cited scholars were Travis Hirschi, David P. Farrington, Michael R. Gottfredson, Alfred Blumstein, and John Braithwaite. An examination of the 50 most-cited scholars in each journal found that only 2 (Farrington and Marvin E. Wolfgang, who was ranked ninth overall) were among the 50 most-cited scholars in all 4 journals, and only Wolfgang was among the 50 most-cited scholars in all 4 journals in both time periods.

During the third time period, 1996–2000 (Cohn & Farrington, 2007a), John Braithwaite, David Garland, David P. Farrington, Richard V. Ericson, and Ken Pease were the most-cited scholars in the 4 major journals. There were no scholars during this time period who were among the most cited in all 4 journals, and only 5 scholars (Braithwaite, Garland, Farrington, Ericson, and the Australian Patrick O'Malley) were among the 50 most cited in 3 of the 4 journals. They also found that scholars who were highly cited in *Criminology* were less likely to be highly cited in the other 3 journals than in the past waves of data, while the number of Australian scholars who were highly cited in 1 of the other 3 journals had increased.

Cohn (2011a; see also Cohn & Farrington, 2012b) examined the fourth wave of data (2001–2005) and found that the most-cited scholars in all 4 journals were David P Farrington, Robert J. Sampson, Travis Hirschi, Michael R. Gottfredson, and Lawrence W. Sherman. Unlike the previous time period, in which no scholar was among the most-cited in all 4 journals, this study found that the 4 most-cited scholars were among the 50 most-cited scholars in all 4 journals and the next 2 (Sherman and Terrie E. Moffitt) were among the most-cited in 3 journals. Cohn (2011a) noted that the average number of cited authors per article was increasing over time, possibly due to the increasing volume of literature in CCJ or the greater availability of full-text materials online (or both). She also found that the 4 journals continued to be parochial, so that the majority of articles published in each journal were written by scholars from their own countries, suggesting that CCJ as a field was not reflecting the increasing globalization of society. The most recent analysis of citations in these 4 major journals, during the years 2006–2010, is reported in Chapter 3.

Cohn and Farrington also looked at the most-cited works of the most-cited authors during each time period, as a way of examining changes and trends in the

Table 1.1 Most-cited works of most-cited scholars in four international journals

	Most-cited scholars	Most-cited works
1986–1990	Marvin E. Wolfgang	*Delinquency in a Birth Cohort* (Wolfgang et al., 1972)
	Alfred Blumstein	*Criminal Careers and "Career Criminals"* (Blumstein et al., 1986)
	David P. Farrington	*The Delinquent Way of Life* (West & Farrington, 1977)
	James Q. Wilson	*Crime and Human Nature* (Wilson & Herrnstein, 1985)
	Stanley Cohen	*Visions of Social Control* (Cohen, 1985)
1991–1995	Travis Hirschi	*A General Theory of Crime* (Gottfredson & Hirschi, 1990)
	David P. Farrington	"Criminal career research: Its value for criminology" (Blumstein et al., 1988)
	Michael R. Gottfredson	*A General Theory of Crime* (Gottfredson & Hirschi, 1990)
	Alfred Blumstein	*Criminal Careers and "Career Criminals"* (Blumstein et al., 1986)
	John Braithwaite	*Crime, Shame, and Reintegration* (Braithwaite, 1989)
1996–2000	John Braithwaite	*Crime, Shame, and Reintegration* (Braithwaite, 1989)
	David Garland	*Punishment and Modern Society* (Garland, 1990)
	David P. Farrington	"The onset and persistence of offending" (Nagin & Farrington, 1992)
	Richard V. Ericson	*Policing the Risk Society* (Ericson & Haggerty, 1997)
	Ken Pease	"Crime placement, displacement, and deflection" (Barr & Pease, 1990)
2001–2005	David P. Farrington	"Life-course trajectories of different types of offenders" (Nagin et al., 1995)
	Robert J. Sampson	*Crime in the Making* (Sampson & Laub, 1993)
	Travis Hirschi	*A General Theory of Crime* (Gottfredson & Hirschi, 1990)
	Michael R. Gottfredson	*A General Theory of Crime* (Gottfredson & Hirschi, 1990)
	Lawrence W. Sherman	*Preventing Crime: What Works, What Doesn't, What's Promising* (Sherman et al., 1997)

focus of criminological research (see Table 1.1). During the 1986–1990 time period (Cohn & Farrington, 1994a), it was clear that longitudinal and criminal career research (Blumstein, Cohen, Roth, & Visher, 1986; West & Farrington, 1977; Wolfgang, Figlio, & Sellin, 1972) was highly influential, along with theoretical research into models of criminal behavior (Hirschi, 1969; Wilson & Herrnstein, 1985). During the 1991–1995 time period (Cohn & Farrington, 1998a; see also Cohn et al., 1998), the most-cited works of the most-cited scholars were more concerned with criminological theories than during the previous wave. The most-cited work of both Hirschi and Gottfredson was *A General Theory of Crime* (Gottfredson & Hirschi, 1990). Farrington's most-cited work was the article "Criminal career research: Its value for criminology" (Blumstein, Cohen, & Farrington, 1988); Blumstein's was *Criminal Careers and "Career Criminals"* (Blumstein et al., 1986); and Braithwaite's was *Crime, Shame, and Reintegration* (Braithwaite, 1989).

Cohn and Farrington's (2007a) examination of citations in 1996–2000 showed an increasing emphasis not only on the causes of crime but also on correctional theories emphasizing ways of dealing with offenders. Braithwaite's most-cited work was, again, *Crime, Shame, and Reintegration* (Braithwaite, 1989); Garland's was *Punishment and Modern Society* (Garland, 1990); Farrington's was the article "The onset and persistence of offending" (Nagin & Farrington, 1992); Ericson's was *Policing the Risk Society* (Ericson & Haggerty, 1997); and Pease's was the article, "Crime placement, displacement, and deflection" (Barr & Pease, 1990). During the final period of 2001–2005 (Cohn & Farrington, 2012b), general theories and life-course research continued to dominate, along with a focus on crime prevention. Farrington's most-cited work during this time period was "Life-course trajectories of different types of offenders" (Nagin, Farrington, & Moffitt, 1995) and Sampson's was *Crime in the Making* (Sampson & Laub, 1993). *A General Theory of Crime* (Gottfredson & Hirschi, 1990) was the most-cited work of both Hirschi and Gottfredson; while Sherman's most-cited work was *Preventing Crime: What Works, What Doesn't, What's Promising* (Sherman et al., 1997).

1.6 Most-Cited Scholars and Works in Six Major American Journals

In addition to their examination of major international CCJ journals, Cohn and Farrington also conducted a series of studies tracing scholarly influence in 3 major American criminology journals (*Criminology*, *Journal of Quantitative Criminology*, and *Journal of Research in Crime and Delinquency*) and 3 major American criminal justice journals (*Justice Quarterly, Journal of Criminal Justice*, and *Criminal Justice and Behavior*). They examined citations in each journal individually, in the 2 groups of journals, and in all 6 journals combined. Cohn and Farrington (1994b) found that the most-cited scholars in the 6 journals in 1986–1990 were Marvin E. Wolfgang, Michael J. Hindelang, Alfred Blumstein, Travis Hirschi, and Michael R. Gottfredson. Of these, only Wolfgang, Hindelang, and Gottfredson were among the most-cited authors in every journal studied. Of the 10 most-cited authors, 9 (all except James Q. Wilson, who was ranked eighth) were relatively more cited in criminology than in criminal justice journals. They also reported that, while there tended to be significant correlations between most of the journals in the most-cited scholars, those scholars who were most-cited in *Criminal Justice and Behavior* were not often highly ranked in any of the other journals.

Cohn and Farrington continued this line of research over subsequent 5-year periods, using the same 6 journals, to examine changes in scholarly influence over time. In the second wave, which covered the years 1991–1995 (Cohn & Farrington, 1998b; see also Cohn et al., 1998), the most-cited scholars in all 6 journals were Travis Hirschi, Michael R. Gottfredson, Robert J. Sampson, Alfred Blumstein, and Lawrence E. Cohen. Only 2 scholars (Hirschi and David P. Farrington) were among the 50 most-cited scholars in all 6 journals; Hirschi was the only scholar ranked in the top 5 in both categories of journals (criminology and criminal justice). As in the previous time period, the majority of the most-cited scholars were relatively more cited in criminology journals; only 4 of the 15 most-cited authors (John L. Hagan, James Q. Wilson, Francis T. Cullen, and Lawrence W. Sherman) were relatively more cited in criminal justice journals.

In the third time period, 1996–2000 (Cohn & Farrington, 2007b), the most-cited scholars in all 6 journals were Travis Hirschi, Michael R. Gottfredson, David P. Farrington, Robert J. Sampson, and Delbert S. Elliott. Hirschi was ranked among the 10 most-cited scholars in each of the 6 journals, and 7 scholars (Hirschi, Gottfredson, Farrington, Elliott, David Huizinga, Douglas A. Smith, and Lawrence W. Sherman) were among the 50 most-cited scholars in all 6 journals. As in the previous waves, the majority of the 20 most-cited scholars were relatively more cited in criminology journals (all except Francis T. Cullen, Wesley G. Skogan, and Lawrence W. Sherman).

The analysis was extended through the years 2001–2005 (Cohn, 2011b), and the most-cited scholars in the 6 journals were found to be David P. Farrington, Robert J. Sampson, Travis Hirschi, Francis T. Cullen, and Raymond Paternoster. Only 4 scholars (Farrington, Cullen, Terrie E. Moffitt, and Rolf Loeber) were ranked among the 50 most-cited scholars in all 6 journals, and 25 of the 30 most-cited scholars (all except Cullen, Harold G. Grasmick, John L. Hagan, Wesley G. Skogan, and Lawrence W. Sherman) were relatively more cited in criminology rather than criminal justice journals. The most recent analysis of citations in these 6 major journals, during the years 2006–2010, is reported in Chapter 4.

An examination of the most-cited works of the most-cited scholars helps to illustrate how the focus and priorities of criminology in the United States has changed over time (see Table 1.2). In 1986–1990, the most-cited works of the most-cited scholars focused primarily on criminal career and longitudinal research (Wolfgang et al., 1972; Blumstein et al., 1986). A particular characteristic of the most-cited works during this time period was that most were books rather than journal articles. During the following time period, 1991–1995 (Cohn & Farrington, 1998b), the most-cited works of the most-cited scholars continued to focus on criminal career and longitudinal research, with an increasing emphasis on theory. Hirschi's most-cited work was *Causes of Delinquency* (Hirschi, 1969); Gottfredson's was *A General Theory of Crime* (Gottfredson & Hirschi, 1990); Sampson's was *Crime in the Making* (Sampson & Laub, 1993); Blumstein's was *Criminal Careers and "Career Criminals"* (Blumstein et al., 1986); and Cohen's was the article "Social change and crime rate trends: A routine activity approach" (Cohen & Felson, 1979).

This trend continued during the third time period, 1996–2000 (Cohn & Farrington, 2007b). *A General Theory of Crime* (Gottfredson & Hirschi, 1990) was both Hirschi and Gottfredson's most-cited work; Farrington's most-cited work was "Age and crime" (Farrington, 1986); Sampson's was *Crime in the Making* (Sampson & Laub, 1993); and Elliott's was *Explaining Delinquency and Drug Use* (Elliott, Huizinga, & Ageton, 1985). In the most recent examination of citations in 2001–2005 (Cohn & Farrington, 2012b), the most-cited works of the most-cited authors again focused on criminal career research and criminological theories. Interestingly, unlike the earlier waves of data, during this time period, the most-cited works were as likely to be articles as books. Farrington's most-cited work in 2001–2005 was "Life-course

1.7 Most-Cited Scholars and Works in 20 Journals

Table 1.2 Most-cited works of most-cited scholars in six American journals

	Most-cited scholars	Most-cited works
1986–1990	Marvin E. Wolfgang	*Delinquency in a Birth Cohort* (Wolfgang et al., 1972)
	Michael J. Hindelang	*Measuring Delinquency* (Hindelang et al., 1981)
	Alfred Blumstein	*Criminal Careers and "Career Criminals"* (Blumstein et al., 1986)
1991–1995	Travis Hirschi	*A General Theory of Crime* (Gottfredson & Hirschi, 1990)
	Michael R. Gottfredson	*A General Theory of Crime* (Gottfredson & Hirschi, 1990)
	Robert J. Sampson	*Crime in the Making* (Sampson & Laub, 1993)
	Alfred Blumstein	*Criminal Careers and "Career Criminals"* (Blumstein et al., 1986)
	Lawrence E. Cohen	"Social changes and crime rate trends" (Cohen & Felson, 1979)
1996–2000	Travis Hirschi	*A General Theory of Crime* (Gottfredson & Hirschi, 1990)
	Michael R. Gottfredson	*A General Theory of Crime* (Gottfredson & Hirschi, 1990)
	David P. Farrington	"Age and crime" (Farrington, 1986)
	Robert J. Sampson	*Crime in the Making* (Sampson & Laub, 1993)
	Delbert S. Elliott	*Explaining Delinquency and Drug Use* (Elliot, Huizinga, & Ageton, 1985)
2001–2005	David P. Farrington	"Life-course trajectories of different types of offenders" (Nagin et al., 1995)
	Robert J. Sampson	*Crime in the Making* (Sampson & Laub, 1993)
	Travis Hirschi	*A General Theory of Crime* (Gottfredson & Hirschi, 1990)
	Francis T. Cullen	"The social dimensions of correctional officer stress" (Cullen et al., 1985)
	Raymond Paternoster	"Using the correct statistical test for the equality of regression coefficients" (Paternoster et al., 1998)

trajectories of different types of offenders" (Nagin et al., 1995); Sampson's was *Crime in the Making* (Sampson & Laub, 1993); Hirschi's was *Measuring Delinquency* (Hindelang, Hirschi, & Weis, 1981); Cullen's was "The empirical status of Gottfredson and Hirschi's general theory of crime" (Pratt & Cullen, 2000); and Paternoster's most-cited work was "Using the correct statistical test for the equality of regression coefficients" (Paternoster, Brame, Mazerolle, & Piquero, 1998).

1.7 Most-Cited Scholars and Works in 20 Journals

One of the concerns with Cohn and Farrington's methodology is that it relies on a relatively small number of mainstream journals and that the results may be biased against scholars working in more specialized areas. To address this, they expanded their methodology to include citations in 20 journals, examining citations from 5 American criminology journals (*Criminology, Journal of Quantitative Criminology, Journal of Research in Crime and Delinquency, Journal of Interpersonal Violence,* and *Violence and Victims*), 5 American criminal justice journals (*Justice Quarterly,*

Journal of Criminal Justice, Crime and Delinquency, Criminal Justice Review, and *Federal Probation*), 5 international criminology journals (*Australian and New Zealand Journal of Criminology; British Journal of Criminology; Canadian Journal of Criminology; Crime, Law, and Social Change;* and *Criminologie*), and 5 international criminal justice journals (*Crime and Justice, Criminal Justice and Behavior, International Journal of Comparative and Applied Criminal Justice, International Journal of Offender Therapy and Comparative Criminology,* and *Social Justice*). Cohn et al. (1998) justified the choice of these 20 journals. Because of the large amount of data involved in this undertaking, citations were only analyzed for 1 year in each journal, beginning in 1990.

Compared with the previous analyses, the expansion to 20 journals benefitted international scholars such as John Braithwaite and Ronald V. Clarke and scholars in less mainstream areas such as Richard J. Gelles (Cohn & Farrington, 1999). In the 1990 analysis, Marvin E. Wolfgang, Travis Hirschi, David P. Farrington, Alfred Blumstein, and Michael R. Gottfredson were the most-cited scholars in 20 journals (Cohn et al., 1998). These results were extremely consistent with those obtained from the studies of 6 American and 4 international journals in 1986–1990. For 1995, Lawrence W. Sherman, Travis Hirschi, Michael R. Gottfredson, David P. Farrington, and Robert J. Sampson were the most-cited scholars, with both Sherman and Sampson having increased citations in the 5-year intervening period (Cohn & Farrington, 1999). One surprising finding was that Marvin E. Wolfgang, who was the most-cited scholar in 1990, was not among the 50 most-cited scholars in 1995.

The most-cited scholars for 2000 were Robert J. Sampson, David P. Farrington, Francis T. Cullen, Travis Hirschi, and Terrie E. Moffitt (Cohn & Farrington, 2008). As in the previous waves of data, there was considerable consistency with the most-cited scholars in the 9 journals during 1996–2000, although there were more highly cited international scholars on the list of most-cited scholars in 20 journals. In 2005, Robert J. Sampson was again the most-cited scholar, followed by John H. Laub, David P. Farrington, Francis T. Cullen, and James L. Bonta (Cohn & Farrington, 2012b). Once again, there was considerable overlap of the most-cited scholars in 20 journals and in the 9 journals studied for the years 2001–2005. It also was clear that international scholars and scholars in less mainstream areas of research tended to be ranked higher in the 20 journal analysis than in the studies examining smaller numbers of journals. The most recent analysis of citations in these 20 journals, in 2010, is reported in Chapter 5.

Cohn and Farrington also looked at the most-cited works of the most-cited authors, as an indicator of the most influential topics in criminological research within each time period (see Table 1.3). The 1990 data (Cohn et al., 1998) revealed the major influence of criminal career research (e.g., Blumstein et al. 1986; Wolfgang et al., 1972) as well as Francis T. Cullen's work on rehabilitation (Cullen & Gilbert, 1982) and Ronald V. Clarke's work on rational choice theory and situational crime prevention (Cornish & Clarke, 1986). By 1995 (Cohn & Farrington, 1999), citations reflected the increasing influence of more general theories of crime and relevant criminal justice policies. Sherman's *Policing Domestic Violence* (Sherman, 1992), Gottfredson and Hirschi's *A General Theory of Crime* (Gottfredson & Hirschi,

1.7 Most-Cited Scholars and Works in 20 Journals

Table 1.3 Most-cited works of most-cited scholars in 20 CCJ journals

	Most-cited scholars	Most-cited works
1990	Marvin E. Wolfgang	*Delinquency in a Birth Cohort* (Wolfgang et al., 1972)
	Travis Hirschi	*Causes of Delinquency* (Hirschi, 1969)
	David P. Farrington	"Criminal career research" (Blumstein et al., 1988)
	Alfred Blumstein	*Criminal Careers and "Career Criminals"* (Blumstein et al., 1986)
	Michael R. Gottfredson	"The true value of lambda would appear to be zero" (Gottfredson & Hirschi, 1986)
1995	Lawrence W. Sherman	*Policing Domestic Violence* (Sherman, 1992)
	Travis Hirschi	*A General Theory of Crime* (Gottfredson & Hirschi, 1990)
	Michael R. Gottfredson	*A General Theory of Crime* (Gottfredson & Hirschi, 1990)
	David P. Farrington	*Understanding and Controlling Crime* (Farrington et al., 1986)
	Robert J. Sampson	*Crime in the Making* (Sampson & Laub, 1993)
2000	Robert J. Sampson	*Crime in the Making* (Sampson & Laub, 1993)
	David P. Farrington	"The development of offending and antisocial behavior from childhood" (Farrington, 1995)
	Francis T. Cullen	"Does correctional treatment work?" (Andrews et al., 1990)
	Travis Hirschi	*A General Theory of Crime* (Gottfredson & Hirschi, 1990)
	Terrie E. Moffitt	"Adolescence-limited and life-course persistent antisocial behavior" (Moffitt, 1993)
2005	Robert J. Sampson	*Crime in the Making* (Sampson & Laub, 1993)
	John H. Laub	*Crime in the Making* (Sampson & Laub, 1993)
	David P. Farrington	"The criminal career paradigm" (Piquero et al., 2003)
	Francis T. Cullen	"Does correctional treatment work?" (Andrews et al., 1990)
	James L. Bonta	*The Psychology of Criminal Conduct* (Andrews & Bonta, 1994, 1998, 2003)

1990), Farrington and colleagues' *Understanding and Controlling Crime* (Farrington, Ohlin, & Wilson, 1986), and *Crime in the Making* (Sampson & Laub, 1993) were the most-cited works in 1995.

Cohn and Farrington's (2008) evaluation of citations in 2000 highlighted a new shift, with increasing numbers of citations of articles in addition to citations of books; the most-cited works of 3 of the 5 most-cited scholars were journal articles. The most-cited works of the most-cited scholars were *Crime in the Making* (Sampson & Laub, 1993), "The development of offending and antisocial behavior from childhood" (Farrington, 1995), "Does correctional treatment work?" (Andrews et al. 1990), *A General Theory of Crime* (Gottfredson & Hirschi, 1990), and "Adolescence-limited and life-course-persistent antisocial behavior" (Moffitt, 1993). In 2005 (Cohn & Farrington, 2012b), the most-cited works of the most-cited scholars illustrated the field's continued attention to life-course and longitudinal research, a topic that remains at the forefront of criminological research today.

1.8 Criminal Career Concepts in Citation Analysis

Cohn and Farrington (1996) argued that concepts originally developed in criminal career research could be employed by citation analysts to enhance understanding of this methodology. They focused particularly on the concepts of prevalence and frequency of citations. There are 2 ways in which a scholar might obtain a large number of citations in a particular journal or group of journals. First, the scholar might have a high prevalence: he or she is cited in many different articles in the target journal(s). A high prevalence of citations could occur either because a small number of works by the scholar are repeatedly cited or because many different works by the scholar are cited only a few times each. Second, the scholar might have a high frequency: many different works by the scholar are cited in only a few articles. In general, Cohn and Farrington (1996) argued that a high prevalence may be a more accurate measure of a scholar's influence on many others in the field because a high frequency of citation may reflect a significant influence on only a small number of other scholars.

Cohn and Farrington (1996) also distinguished between specialization and versatility. A specialized author has a small number of works (possibly only 1 or 2) that are frequently cited; these works are often books that present a major theory. Versatile authors are those that have many different works cited, with no single seminal work standing out as being particularly highly cited. It is possible to be both specialized and versatile, i.e., having 1 highly cited seminal work as well as having a wide variety of different works cited. A high frequency of citation *must* be associated with versatility, while a high prevalence *may be* (but is not always) associated with specialization; a versatile author could have a high prevalence if a large number of the scholar's works were cited in many different articles in the journal. This would also indicate a great influence on other researchers.

1.9 Limitations of Citation Analysis

While the use of citation analysis to study scholarly prestige and influence has some notable advantages, particularly the objective and quantitative nature of the research, some concerns have been raised (see Cohn & Farrington, 2012b for a more detailed discussion). One of the most frequent objections is the claim that citation analysis emphasizes quantity rather than quality. However, research has consistently found correlations between citation counts and other measures of scholarly influence, including peer ratings (see, e.g., Myers, 1970), scholarly awards and recognition (see, e.g., Myers, 1970; Rushton & Endler, 1979; Cole & Cole, 1971), and scholarly productivity and publication rates (see, e.g., Gordon & Vicari, 1992).

Another issue is that citation counts may be biased against those scholars working in very specialized and less popular areas. While these researchers may be extremely influential in their own areas, the limited number of others working in that specialty area may mean that these scholars are less likely to be highly cited in mainstream journals (Chapman, 1989). It has also been suggested that methodological papers are likely to be highly cited (see, e.g., Peritz, 1983; Douglas, 1992). However, in their longitudinal studies of citations, Cohn and Farrington found that books and articles focusing on research methodology were rarely among the most-cited works of the most-cited scholars.

Chapman (1989) argued that citation analysis does not allow scholars to differentiate between citations that are positive, negative, or neutral, pointing out that "Citation does not necessarily denote approval" (Chapman, 1989, p. 341). However, it appears that the vast majority of citations are either positive or neutral (see, e.g., Cole, 1975; Garfield, 1979; Cohn & Farrington, 1994a). Additionally, as Cohn and Farrington (1994a) pointed out, if a researcher takes the time and effort to formally criticize a scholarly work in print, that work clearly has had some influence on that researcher.

1.10 Conclusion

This chapter has reviewed the use of citation analysis, especially the research conducted by Cohn and Farrington, and its contributions to the body of criminological literature and to the study of scholarly prestige and influence. For more detailed reviews of the use of citation analysis in CCJ and other disciplines, see Cohn and Farrington (2012b).

This book presents the most recent analysis of citations in CCJ using the methods developed by Cohn and Farrington. Chapter 2 describes the methodology being used in detail. Chapters 3, 4, and 5 examine the most-cited scholars and works in 4 international journals, 6 American CCJ journals, and 20 American and international journals, respectively. Finally, Chapter 6 discusses the policy implications of this research and future research on citation analysis.

Chapter 2
Methodology

2.1 Selecting a Source of Citation Data

In their early research, Cohn and Farrington (1994a, 1994b) decided to obtain citation data from a small number of prestigious journals in criminology and criminal justice (CCJ) rather than using data from larger sources such as the Social Science Citation Index (SSCI). At that time (1986–1990), SSCI was only available in print format, although today it is part of Thomson Reuters' online *Web of Science* (WoS). While this resource provides access to citations in a large number of social science journals in a variety of disciplines, it also has some significant disadvantages. Some of the problems in the print version of SSCI have been corrected by the conversion to electronic format, but a number remain. WoS includes self-citations, which need to be excluded if the purpose of the research is to examine 1 scholar's influence on others in the field. Additionally, any errors present in journal reference lists, such as spelling mistakes or incorrect initials, are carried over and reproduced in the WoS. If the journal permits the use of the generic "et al." in the reference list, those additional authors will not be included in the WoS.

The list of journals used by the WoS is not fixed; new journals are constantly being added and older ones removed from the master journal list. The WoS website includes a list of "Journal Coverage Changes," listing all journal changes over the past 12 months. In March 2013, this list ran to 26 single-spaced pages, with over 40 journals per page (Thomson Reuters, 2013). This clearly makes longitudinal research extremely difficult, if not impossible. The database is primarily limited to journals and a very small number of book series; in general, citations from books and book chapters are not included. This may result in a significant bias, especially in fields like criminology and criminal justice, where books appear to be highly significant (Cohn & Farrington, 1994b).

As many journal reference lists only include the last names and first initials of the authors, the WoS listings also may merge the citations of multiple scholars with the same surname and first initials; for example, a search for "J. Cohen" brings up not only citations to works by Jacqueline Cohen but also citations of Joseph and Jacob

Cohen. Similarly, "P. Brantingham" produces works by both Patricia and Paul Brantingham. The problem is compounded by scholars who have the same first name as well (e.g., the multiple Richard Berks or David Smiths) or who use middle initials that may be omitted in the reference lists (e.g., Ellen G. and Ellen S. Cohn).

Other current sources of citation data are online scientific archives such as Google Scholar and Elsevier's Scopus, both of which began operations in 2004. Google Scholar (GS) is a free online scientific archive that trawls full-text journals and bibliographic databases and includes citations from not only journal articles and books but also technical reports, court opinions, theses, and a number of "scholarly" web pages. In general, GS tends to produce more citations than WoS (Bauer & Bakkalbasi, 2005; Meho & Yang, 2007). However, there are a number of concerns regarding the software used by GS (see, e.g., Jascó, 2008a, 2008b, 2009a, 2009b). It is also impossible to obtain information on the coverage of the database, such as which journals are included, which databases are trawled, which time periods are covered, or how often GS is updated (Cohn & Farrington, 2012b). Additionally, self-citations are included in GS.

Scopus is a fee-based abstract and citation database operated by Elsevier. As of November 2012, it contained over 20,500 active titles from over 5,000 international publishers, including about 18,500 peer-reviewed journals, 400 trade publications, 360 book series, and 5.3 million conference papers from journals and proceedings, as well as articles in press from over 3,850 journals. This totaled approximately 49 million records. Scopus also includes approximately 376 million scientific-indexed web pages and almost 25 million patent records (Scopus, 2013). While it is very user friendly and fast, there are a number of limitations of Scopus (see, e.g., Dess, 2006). Over 40 % of the records (21 million) are from before 1996 and do not include references; only those records from 1996 onwards (28 million) include cited references (Scopus, 2013). This greatly limits citation tracking and longitudinal research. Additionally, the number of records identified by a search varies depending on the order in which search terms are entered, especially if the "search within" function is used (Dess, 2006).

The third option open to citation analysis researchers is to directly examine the reference lists of journals and books in a given field and to count the number of citations of a given scholar, work, or journals. While this method is significantly more time consuming than using online databases, it avoids many of the problems inherent in their use. Cohn and Farrington developed and used this method successfully in their early research (e.g., Cohn & Farrington, 1990, 1994a, 1994b, 1996; Wright & Cohn, 1996). This method is objective, quantitative, transparent, and replicable, as the raw data are available to any researcher with access to the chosen journals and their reference lists.

2.2 Journal Selection

Selecting the specific journals to be studied was the first step in the research process. Cohn and Farrington began this line of research in the late 1980s, so, while both American and international journals were considered, the journals were chosen based on the needs of the specific research projects that they were conducting at that time. Additionally, because of language limitations, they limited themselves to journals published primarily (although not necessarily completely) in English.

Journal selection was, of course, limited to journals being published in 1986, so newer journals such as *Criminology and Public Policy*, the *European Journal of Criminology*, and the *Journal of Experimental Criminology* which were not then in print were not possible sources of citation data at that time. As this is a longitudinal study, it is not possible to add or remove journals from the study and still have results that may be compared to those obtained in earlier waves.

There are a wide variety of journals that publish articles in CCJ but which focus predominantly on other fields, such as sociology (e.g., *Social Forces, American Sociological Review*, and *Social Problems*), child and adolescent psychology and psychopathology (e.g., *Development and Psychopathology, Journal of Adolescence*, and the *Journal of Youth and Adolescence*), legal/social issues (e.g., *Law and Human Behavior, Law and Social Inquiry, Behavioral Sciences and the Law*, and *Law and Society Review*), and so on (see Vaughn, del Carmen, Perfecto, & Charand, 2004, for an extremely useful annotated list of 326 journals relating to CCJ). While it is possible that scholars who were initially trained in a cognate discipline and who conduct research in CCJ may prefer to publish some or all of their research in the mainstream journals of their original discipline, we chose to focus on journals that are centrally concerned with CCJ.

There are also many specialized journals within criminal justice that publish on very specific topics within the field. These include journals such as *Homicide Studies, Journal of Threat Assessment, Juvenile and Family Court Journal, Policing: An International Journal of Police Strategies and Management, Child Maltreatment*, and the *American Journal of Drug and Alcohol Abuse*. While these and other specialist journals publish many extremely important works, we chose not to include them in our analyses because their focus is very narrow and they do not encompass the entire field of CCJ. Our research is focused on mainstream CCJ journals.

2.3 Selecting Four International Journals

The original research (Cohn & Farrington, 1990) used citations to examine differences between criminology in the United States and the United Kingdom by comparing citations in 2 key criminology journals, *Criminology* (CRIM) and the *British Journal of Criminology* (BJC). CRIM is the official journal of the American Society of Criminology (ASC) and is sent to all members, giving it an extremely wide circulation and increasing the likelihood that articles in this journal will be noticed and read by American criminologists more than articles in other American criminology journals. BJC, published by Oxford University Press, is unambiguously the leading criminological journal in the United Kingdom.

Their analysis was later expanded to include the leading peer-reviewed criminology journals in other English-speaking countries—specifically Canada, Australia, and New Zealand (Cohn & Farrington, 1994a). The leading criminological journal in Canada is the *Canadian Journal of Criminology and Criminal Justice* (CJC), formerly the *Canadian Journal of Criminology*, which is published by the Canadian Criminal Justice Association. While this journal is published partly in French, many articles are in English and those that are not in English include an English abstract. The primary journal in Australia and New Zealand is the *Australian and New Zealand Journal of Criminology* (ANZ), which is published by the Australian and New Zealand Society of Criminology and sent to all members of the society.

2.4 Selecting Six American Journals

Cohn and Farrington's next study involved an examination of citations in major American CCJ journals (Cohn & Farrington, 1994b), which they limited to CCJ journals with American editors and publishers. Journals with significant international content and journals published and edited outside the United States were excluded from this analysis. Three of the journals they selected were centrally concerned with criminology—CRIM, the *Journal of Quantitative Criminology* (JQC), and the *Journal of Research in Crime and Delinquency* (JRCD). The other three were centrally concerned with criminal justice—*Justice Quarterly* (JQ), the *Journal of Criminal Justice* (JCJ), and *Criminal Justice and Behavior* (CJB).

A review of the literature available at the time provided considerable empirical evidence to support the claim that these were among the most prestigious American journals in CCJ. Shichor, O'Brien, and Decker (1981) asked American criminologists to rank American and international journals containing articles on CCJ and found that the *Journal of Criminal Law and Criminology* (JCLC) had the highest average rating, followed by CRIM and JRCD. JCJ was ranked fifth in the survey, after *Crime and Delinquency* (CD). The next most highly-ranked American CCJ journals were *Criminal Justice Review* (CJR), *Federal Probation* (FP), and CJB. A similar but much larger survey conducted by Regoli, Poole, and Miracle (1982) found that the most highly-ranked and prestigious CCJ journals were CRIM, JRCD, JCLC, CD, JCJ, and CJB. A survey of criminal justice professionals (rather than academic criminologists) conducted by Fabianic (1980) obtained similar results, finding that the most highly-ranked journals were JCLC, JCJ, CRIM, and JRCD. Parker and Goldfeder's (1979) survey of heads of graduate programs found that the most highly-ranked CCJ journals were JCLC, CRIM, CD, JCJ, FP, JRCD, and CJB.

Citation analysis also supports the selection of these journals as among the most prestigious American CCJ journals. Poole and Regoli's (1981) study of journal citations in CRIM between 1975 and 1979 found that citation-based rankings of journals were highly correlated (rank correlation=0.75) with the subjective rankings obtained by Shichor et al. (1981); based on citations, the most highly-ranked journals were JCLC, CRIM, CD, JRCD, and FP. After controlling for the number of articles available to be cited, Cohn and Farrington (1990) found that the most-cited journals in CRIM between 1984 and 1988 were CRIM, JCLC, JRCD, CD, JCJ, and CJB. Stack's (1987) research using SSCI also controlled for the number of articles that could be cited and found that the most-cited American CCJ journals were CRIM, JRCD, CD, JCLC, CJB, and JCJ.

Although these studies found that CD, FP, and JCLC were considered to be among the most important American CCJ journals, Cohn and Farrington did not use these journals in their research. Almost half of the issues in CD were special issues that include solicited articles on specific topics rather than unsolicited articles on general topics in CCJ. FP is a specialist journal focusing specifically on probation, rather than a general journal presenting topics spanning the field of CCJ. The legal style of footnoting used by JCLC in the 1980s used only the last names of the authors cited, omitting initials and therefore making it nearly impossible to determine the identity of authors who shared the same surname. Although JCLC now includes the first name or initials of authors, the footnote style of citation still makes it extremely difficult to obtain citation information. Because footnotes appear throughout an article (as opposed to collecting references at the end of the article), Cohn and Farrington would have had to search through each article for those footnotes that contained references, identify and delete any extraneous material in the footnote, and then copy each reference to a new file. As JCLC begins references with first names, each reference would have to be individually edited to reverse the first and last names so that references could be sorted by last name. Additionally, Sorensen (2009) found that a large percentage of articles in JCLC deal with topics relating to criminal law rather than criminal justice and/or criminology.

Both JQ and JQC were not listed among the most prestigious journals in many of these early studies because they did not begin publishing until 1984 and 1985, respectively. However, by the time Cohn and Farrington began their research, they believed them to be more prestigious than several of the other journals identified by the earlier research (e.g., *Criminal Justice Review*, *Journal of Crime and Justice*). JCJ was, and JQ is, the house journal of the Academy of Criminal Justice Sciences (ACJS).

2.5 Selecting 20 American and International Journals

The selection process described above resulted in a total of 9 CCJ journals: 3 American criminology journals (CRIM, JQC, and JRCD), 3 American criminal justice journals (JQ, JCJ, and CJB), and 3 international journals (ANZ, BJC, and CJC). In a separate study, Cohn and Farrington also examined citations in *Crime and Justice: A Review of Research* (CAJ) (Cohn & Farrington, 1996), bringing the total number of publications studied to ten. While these are all well-known, high-quality, peer-reviewed publications, Cohn and Farrington were concerned that the limited number of journals studied could potentially create a bias against scholars who publish in less mainstream or slightly lower-tier journals as it could be argued that the results might vary depending on the particular journals being analyzed.

They therefore decided to investigate the most-cited scholars in a much larger number of American and international CCJ journals (Cohn, Farrington, & Wright

1998), doubling the number of journals studied from 10 to 20. As they had already been assessing American and international journals and comparing criminology and criminal justice journals, Cohn and Farrington decided to examine 5 journals in each of four possible groupings: American criminology journals, American criminal justice journals, international criminology journals, and international criminal justice journals. Selecting the additional 10 journals was a difficult undertaking.

Cohn and Farrington first eliminated nonacademic publications such as *The Police Chief* and *Corrections Today*, as well as mainstream academic journals in cognate disciplines (e.g., psychology, psychiatry, sociology, economics, drug and alcohol studies), and then considered a wide variety of academic journals. Some prestigious journals such as the *Journal of Crime and Justice* and the *Howard Journal of Criminal Justice* had too few citations to be reasonably analyzed. In 1990, the most-cited scholar in the *Journal of Crime and Justice* had only four citations, and only 3 scholars had 4 or more citations in the *Howard Journal of Criminal Justice* in 1990. Others were on specific topics within CCJ (e.g., *Victimology, Policing, The Prison Journal, Criminal Justice History, Police Studies*) or focused primarily on related disciplines such as legal psychology, socio-legal studies, and the sociology of deviance.

They eventually selected 10 additional CCJ journals: CD, *Criminal Justice Review* (CJR), FP, *Criminologie* (CRGE), *Contemporary Crises* (now renamed *Crime, Law and Social Change*: CLSC), the *International Journal of Comparative and Applied Criminal Justice* (IJCA), the *International Journal of Offender Therapy and Comparative Criminology* (IJOT), *Journal of Interpersonal Violence* (JIV), *Social Justice* (SJ), and *Violence and Victims* (VAV). As the original research using these 20 journals was conducted in 1990, they used data from that year to classify journals as American or international. Of the 5 journals we identified as international criminology journals, 4 (ANZ, BJC, CJC, and CRGE) were published outside the United States and contained very few American authors, while the fifth, CLSC, was at that time subtitled "An International Journal" and was published in the Netherlands. In 2005, only 18 % of the authors in CLSC were American, and the journal included 14 non-Americans out of 27 editors, senior editors, and associate editors.

One of the 5 international criminal justice journals, IJCA, is the official journal of the American Society of Criminology's Division of International Criminology and is explicitly international in its focus. The second, IJOT, "a journal of international cooperation," is also explicitly international in its focus and included 29 non-Americans out of 56 consulting and associate editors in 2005. SJ, a project of "Global Options," included an international editorial advisory board drawn from 13 countries in addition to the United States in 2005. CJB, the official publication of the International Association for Correctional and Forensic Psychology, is subtitled "An International Journal," and the journal information clearly states that "articles… are welcomed from throughout the world." CAJ, according to its promotional material, has, "since 1979 […] presented a review of the latest international research." Its editor, Michael H. Tonry, was located in the United Kingdom in 1999–2004, and currently has an affiliation in the Netherlands.

For the original 9 journals, Cohn and Farrington obtained citations for each year of publication and studied them in 5-year periods (beginning with the earliest study that examined citations in 1986–1990). However, the extensive amount of work involved in the process of data collection was too great to permit annual data collection for all 20 journals; therefore, they only analyzed 1 year of data out of each 5-year period (beginning with 1990).

2.6 Obtaining the Citation Data

The citation data were obtained from the reference lists in each article in each of the journals. We defined articles as including not only research articles but research notes, comments, and rejoinders. We excluded book reviews, book review articles, editorials, introductions to special issues, letters, and obituaries. The reference pages for each article had to be entered into the computer. Originally, Cohn and Farrington did this by photocopying the reference lists, scanning them into the computer with an optical scanner and OCR software, and editing the resulting text to correct the large number of typographical errors created by the scanning process. Today, however, the increasing prevalence of full-text online journals allows us the ability to download references from most journals directly into a word processing program for editing, significantly streamlining the data entry process by not only reducing the time and cost of the process but also greatly decreasing errors in the reference lists. In addition to downloading journal reference lists, we also print out the title page and reference pages of each article, as well as the table of contents for each journal issue. Using this material for cross-checking helps to ensure that no articles or references have been omitted.

After downloading the reference lists, the citations had to be converted into a format that was suitable for analysis. For references with multiple authors, this involved making duplicate listings of the reference with each individual coauthor listed first in one of the listings. This was extremely labor-intensive but was essential as it ensured that all coauthors received equal credit for being cited, rather than only acknowledging the first author (this was a serious problem with SSCI until recently). Self-citations were identified and marked for later exclusion, and institutional authors (e.g., Home Office, National Institute of Justice, *New York Times*) were removed from the data set. In journals such as CJB that permit the use of "et al." in the reference list, the names of the additional coauthors were, when possible, obtained and included in the data. All cited authors received equal credit; citation counts were not inversely weighted according to the number of coauthors (this is more common in publication productivity studies such as Rice, Cohn, & Farrington 2005; Steiner & Schwartz, 2006; Shutt & Barnes, 2008). Restricting the study to published works was not feasible so all works cited were included (e.g., unpublished papers, theses and dissertations, conference presentations). Self-citations were excluded from analysis, although coauthor citations were noted but included (Cohn & Farrington, 1996). These occur when the author of an article cites one of his or her own multiauthored works. For example, if Robert J. Sampson publishes an article in CRIM in which he cites a work he coauthored with John H. Laub, Laub is a coauthor citation. In that situation, Laub would be credited with a citation but Sampson would not.

We carried out an extensive amount of checking to ensure that no references were omitted, that all self-citations were identified and excluded, that typographical errors were minimized, and to detect and if possible correct mistakes in the original reference lists (which were unfortunately extremely common). This process involved careful cross-checking using the photocopied pages of the reference lists. For each article, we counted the number of cited authors in the reference list and identified self-citations and coauthor citations. This information was compared with the corresponding information in the computer file and any discrepancies were identified and corrected. We also compiled information on the total number of authors cited in each article, the number of self-citations, and the number of coauthor citations. This permitted us to compute the number of "eligible" citations by subtracting the number of self-citations in an article from the total number of authors cited in that article. We also recorded the number of authors of each article and the nationality of each author. Nationality was defined by the country of the institution with which an author was affiliated; when an author listed multiple affiliations in different countries, the first-listed institution was used. For those authors with no institutional affiliation, their geographic location was used.

2.7 Counting Citations

After completing the editing process for an individual journal, the list of citations was sorted into alphabetical order and put into a spreadsheet. This was then examined to determine the number of times each scholar was cited; the previously identified self-citations were noted but not included in a scholar's total citation count.

This process was often very difficult because, in many journals, the reference lists include only last names and initials rather than full names, creating confusion when there are multiple scholars with the same last name and initials; this problem was compounded even further in situations where middle initials were omitted. In those cases, references were cross-checked against the original source publications to distinguish between, for example, the various D. Smiths (David A, David E., David J., Douglas A., etc.), the various J. Cohens (Jacqueline, Jacob, Joseph, etc.), and the 2 P. Brantinghams (Paul J. and Patricia L.). In addition, there are several cases where 2 scholars share the same name (e.g., David Brown, Richard Sparks, Richard Wright, Patrick O'Malley); in those situations it was necessary to examine the complete citation listings carefully to distinguish between them. Citations to scholars with multiple names (e.g., Kimberly Kempf/Leonard) also had to be amalgamated, when they were known.

We also had to check and correct a distressingly large number and variety of errors made in the original reference lists. Authors' names were often misspelled (e.g., T. Hirsch or T. Hirshi instead of T. Hirschi, D.P. Farringdon instead of D.P.

Farrington, R. Lober instead of R. Loeber) and initials were often omitted or were incorrect (e.g., J. Sampson or R.A. Sampson instead of R.J. Sampson, A.P. Piquero instead of A.R. Piquero). This was a difficult task and one that required considerable knowledge of the field. Our extensive experience in citation analysis often enabled us to easily determine from the title of an article or the coauthors that, for example, a citation to "R.A. Sampson" really referred to "R.J. Sampson" or a citation to "K. Cohen" really referred to "J. Cohen." However, someone with less familiarity with the criminology literature might not recognize these errors and might instead carry them over into the citation count data. Of course, they would also be carried over in any mechanical analysis of citations using internet sources such as Google Scholar and Scopus. While it is unlikely that we were able to correct every error in every reference list, we are confident that we were able to detect and correct the vast majority of them, particularly those involving the most-cited authors in each journal.

As has been noted, citation analysis is both objective and quantitative. Another advantage is that the raw data are readily available to anyone with access to the journals, making this research highly replicable. However, it is important to realize that 1 year of citations in a journal such as JCJ may include over 15,000 cited authors to be checked and counted. In total, we analyzed over 500,000 cited authors in 9 journals from 1986 to 2010. Therefore, it is possible that another researcher may fail to exactly replicate our results because of mistakes in the spelling of authors' names that have not been detected by these authors or by the other researcher, difficulties in distinguishing between authors with the same surname and first initial, possible inconsistencies in the definition of "article," or because of minor and infrequent clerical errors that may creep into such a large data set, despite extremely careful checking. However, the prevalence of and large support for the previous Cohn and Farrington research suggests that our main conclusions would hold up with only marginal changes in any replication.

Once the citation data were counted and checked, the 50 most-cited scholars in each journal were identified and ranked; when multiple scholars had the same number of citations in a specific journal, they were given the same average ranking. We also determined the number of different works cited and the number of different articles in which the most-cited scholars were cited; this provided measures of prevalence, frequency, specialization, and versatility (see the discussion of career concepts in citation analysis in Chapter 1). These rankings were compared to those obtained during earlier waves of research to provide information about changes in an individual scholar's influence on others in the field.

2.8 Limitations of This Methodology

There are a number of limitations of this type of citation analysis research, many of which are attributable to the longitudinal design being employed. First, it is based on citations in a relatively small number of mainstream CCJ journals. Scholars who publish in journals that focus on cognate disciplines, such as sociology or psychology, or who publish in more specialized CCJ journals that focus on a narrow area within the field may not be highly cited in the journals studied, and their influence may be underestimated.

Second, because this is a longitudinal study, only those journals that existed at the time the research began could be used (1986 for the 9 major international and American CCJ journals and 1990 for the expanded 20 journal study). Journals that were not then being published, such as *Criminology and Public Policy*, the *European Journal of Criminology*, or the *Journal of Experimental Criminology*, cannot be incorporated into the study.

Third, because of the longitudinal design, the research cannot be revised to take advantage of the many new sources of citation data such as the Web of Science, Scopus, and Google Scholar. Similarly, the methods of analyzing the citation data cannot be changed. For example, while our method has eliminated self-citations, coauthor citations are included in the data. While it would be interesting and possibly instructive to look at the impact of coauthor citations on rankings, it is not possible at this point to remove those citations.

2.9 Strengths of This Methodology

Although the longitudinal design of this research does result in a number of limitations, it is also one of the primary strengths of this research methodology. This study is based on citation data collected from major CCJ journals over a period of 25 years. Because electronic sources of citation data did not exist when this research began, it would not be possible to carry out such a long-term study based on those data sources. Secondly, this research used the same set of journals throughout. Electronic sources of citation data are constantly changing the source journals from which they obtain citation data, making it almost impossible to obtain comparable longitudinal data.

Another important strength of this research is the careful and extensive checking of the data that was carried out in an effort to locate and correct the many errors that appear in the original reference lists, such as misspelled authors' names, incorrect or omitted initials, and incorrect reference dates. When online sources of citation data are used, these errors remain because citations are not checked for accuracy. We conducted a detailed examination, informed by an extensive and in-depth knowledge of the literature and the individual scholars in CCJ, that, while it may not have corrected every error, clearly corrected many that would otherwise have been missed.

Fourth, this research excludes self-citations, which do not indicate a scholar's influence on others in the field. Online sources of citation data do not do this; nor do they clearly identify self-citations so that they can be extracted manually.

Finally, while it may be argued that the limited number of journals examined under our method is a limitation, it is also a strength of this research. All the journals being studied are well-regarded, prestigious, and widely read mainstream journals in CCJ. More general sources of citation data, such as Web of Science or Scopus, would collect citations from a wider variety of journals but would include trade publications as well as journals that are less prestigious or that are only peripherally associated with CCJ, thus significantly diluting the validity of the conclusions.

2.10 The Current Research

The original analysis developing the Cohn and Farrington methodology was a study of citations in 4 major international criminology journals during the years 1986–1990 (Cohn & Farrington, 1994a). This was then extended over the next three 5-year periods: 1991–1995 (Cohn et al., 1998; Cohn & Farrington, 1998a), 1996–2000 (Cohn & Farrington, 2007a), and 2001–2005 (Cohn, 2011a; see also Cohn & Farrington, 2012b). The analysis of 6 major American CCJ journals also originally examined citations during the period 1986–1990 (Cohn & Farrington, 1994b) and continued through the next 3 time periods: 1991–1995 (Cohn & Farrington, 1998b; see also Cohn et al., 1998), 1996–2000 (Cohn & Farrington, 2007b), and 2001–2005 (Cohn, 2011b; see also Cohn & Farrington, 2012b). This research extends these analyses through 2006–2010 and analyzes longitudinal trends in scholarly influence over the 25-year period. Cohn and Farrington's analysis of 20 major journals originally covered the year 1990 (Cohn et al., 1998) and was later extended to cover the years 1995 (Cohn & Farrington, 1999), 2000 (Cohn & Farrington, 2008), and 2005 (Cohn & Farrington, 2012a). This work extends this to the year 2010 and also examines changes in scholarly influence over time.

Chapter 3
Most-Cited Scholars in Four International Journals

As discussed in Chapter 2, Cohn and Farrington's original research focused on citations in major English-speaking countries and examined the most-cited scholars in the major international criminology and criminal justice (CCJ) journals of 5 countries: *Australian and New Zealand Journal of Criminology* (ANZ), *British Journal of Criminology* (BJC), *Canadian Journal of Criminology and Criminal Justice* (CJC), and *Criminology* (CRIM), which is the house journal of the American Society of Criminology. In this chapter, we extend that analysis to the most recent time period, 2006–2010. The most-cited works of the most-cited scholars are also listed. Comparisons are made with 4 earlier time periods (1986–1990, 1991–1995, 1996–2000, and 2001–2005) so that changes in the influence and prestige of scholars during the past 25 years can be documented.

3.1 *Australian and New Zealand Journal of Criminology* (ANZ)

In ANZ in 2006–2010, 101 articles were published by a total of 212 authors (not necessarily different authors, since 1 individual scholar could be an author or coauthor on more than 1 article); 57 % of authors (120) were located in Australia and 6 % (12) were located in New Zealand. The other authors were most commonly from the United States (48) or the United Kingdom (17). While the number of articles published in this time period did not change significantly compared to the last time period (108 articles in 2001–2005), there was an increase in the number of authors (from 194 in 2001–2005).

These articles contained a total of 9,576 cited authors, of which 527 were self-citations and 437 were coauthor citations. The 9,049 eligible cited authors (an average of 90 cited authors per article) may be compared with 7,083 in 2001–2005 (66 per article), 4,592 in 1996–2000 (45 per article), 3,833 in 1991–1995 (39 per article), and 3,620 in 1986–1990 (43 per article). Although the number of cited authors per article was fairly stable in the earlier time periods, it increased markedly in 2001–2005 and 2006–2010 and is now twice the number seen in 1986–1990.

Table 3.1 shows the most-cited scholars in ANZ in 2006–2010 (those with ranks up to 50). Because there were 8 scholars with tied ranks of 48.5, there are actually 52 names in this table. The most-cited scholar, Robert J. Sampson, was cited 76 times. He was quite versatile, with 41 different works cited in 26 different articles (26 % of all ANZ articles). His most-cited work, *Crime in the Making* (Sampson & Laub, 1993), was cited only ten times. The second most-cited scholar, David P. Farrington, was cited 63 times. The highest-ranked female scholars were Terrie E. Moffitt (ranked 15) and Kathleen Daly (16). Editors of journals are indicated in the tables in case their citations are enhanced by their editorship (because article authors may wish to curry favor with editors).

Table 3.1 also shows the comparable rankings of these scholars in ANZ in the 4 earlier time periods. Lawrence W. Sherman was the most-cited scholar in 2001–2005, and his most-cited work in that time period was *Preventing Crime* (Sherman et al., 1997). John Braithwaite was the most-cited scholar in both 1996–2000 and 1991–1995; his most-cited work in both time periods was *Crime, Shame, and Reintegration* (Braithwaite, 1989). Richard G. Fox was the most-cited scholar in 1986–1990, and his most-cited work then was *Sentencing* (Fox & Freiberg, 1985).

Twenty-nine of the most-cited scholars in 2006–2010 (56 %) had been ranked in the top 50 in 2001–2005, but only 14 (27 %) had been ranked in the top 50 in 1996–2000, 12 (23 %) in 1991–1995, and 10 (19 %) in 1986–1990. Only John Braithwaite, Janet B. L. Chan, Arie Freiberg, and Stanley Cohen were ranked in the top 50 in all 5 time periods; 7 additional scholars were ranked in the top 50 in 4 of the 5 time periods. John Braithwaite was ranked in the most-cited 3 or 4 scholars in all 5 time periods. Between 2001–2005 and 2006–2010, big advances were made by John H. Laub (from 20.5 to 6.5), Don Weatherburn (from 34.5 to 8), and Chris Cunneen (from 50 to 9). The highest new entrants in the table were Daniel S. Nagin (4.5), Raymond Paternoster (4.5), and Alex R. Piquero (6.5). Moving downwards in rank between 2001–2005 and 2006–2010 were Kathleen Daly (from 4 to 16), David Garland (from 6 to 22), and Lawrence W. Sherman (from 1 to 26). Seven of the 10 most-cited scholars in 2001–2005 survived to be in the 50 most-cited scholars in 2006–2010: all except Jock Young (ranked 7 in 2001–2005), Heather Strang (9), and Ross J. Homel (10).

3.2 British Journal of Criminology (BJC)

In BJC in 2006–2010, 240 articles were published by a total of 414 individual authors, 50 % of whom (205) were from the United Kingdom. The other authors were most commonly from the United States (74), Australia (31), Canada (27), and the Netherlands (23). The number of articles, but not the number of authors, increased from the previous time period (217 articles and 417 individual authors in 2001–2005).

Table 3.1 Most-cited scholars in *Australian and New Zealand Journal of Criminology*

Rank in 2006–2010	Rank in 2001–2005	Rank in 1996–2000	Rank in 1991–1995	Rank in 1986–1990	Name	Cites
1	5	–	–	–	Robert J. Sampson	76
2	3	–	29.5	43	David P. Farrington	63
3	2	1	1	3.5	John Braithwaite	39
4.5	–	–	–	–	Daniel S. Nagin	38
4.5	–	–	–	–	Raymond Paternoster	38
6.5	20.5	–	–	–	John H. Laub	34
6.5	–	–	–	–	Alex R. Piquero	34
8	34.5	–	–	–	Don Weatherburn	32
9	50	4.5	9.5	–	Chris Cunneen	30
10	–	–	–	–	Tom R. Tyler	27
12	26	–	–	32.5	Alfred Blumstein	25
12	16.5	–	–	43	Travis Hirschi	25
12	–	4.5	–	–	Ken Pease	25
14	–	45	–	–	Julian V. Roberts	24
15	20.5	–	–	–	Terrie E. Moffitt	23
16	4	–	–	–	Kathleen Daly	22
17	50	–	–	–	J. David Hawkins	21
19	–	–	–	–	Francis T. Cullen	20
19	26	–	–	–	David Indermauer	20
19	8	7.5	35.5	–	John Pratt[a]	20
22	–	–	–	–	Robert Brame	18
22	6	2	12	–	David Garland	18
22	–	–	–	–	Rolf Loeber	18
26	34.5	–	–	–	Ronald V. Clarke	17
26	20.5	22.5	–	21	Allison Morris	17
26	11	–	17.5	–	Clifford D. Shearing	17
26	1	29.5	17.5	–	Lawrence W. Sherman	17
26	–	–	–	–	Darrell J. Steffensmeier	17
30	34.5	22.5	45.5	21	Janet B.L. Chan	16
30	34.5	–	–	–	Michael R. Gottfredson	16
30	–	26	–	–	Gabrielle Maxwell	16
33	50	–	–	–	Marcus Felson	15
33	20.5	35.5	15	6.5	Arie Freiberg	15
33	16.5	–	–	–	Bronwyn Lind	15
39.5	–	–	–	–	Michael W. Arthur	14
39.5	50	–	45.5	32.5	Anthony E. Bottoms	14
39.5	–	16	24	–	Roderic G. Broadhurst	14
39.5	50	–	–	–	Richard F. Catalano	14
39.5	34.5	–	–	21	Jacqueline Cohen	14
39.5	–	35.5	–	–	J. Michael Hough	14
39.5	–	–	–	–	David Huizinga	14
39.5	–	–	–	–	Stephen W. Raudenbush	14
39.5	–	–	–	–	Richard E. Tremblay	14

(continued)

Table 3.1 (continued)

Rank in 2006–2010	Rank in 2001–2005	Rank in 1996–2000	Rank in 1991–1995	Rank in 1986–1990	Name	Cites
39.5	–	–	–	–	Per-Olof Wikstrom	14
48.5	–	–	–	–	Patricia L. Brantingham	13
48.5	–	–	–	–	Paul J. Brantingham	13
48.5	50	7.5	8	3.5	Stanley Cohen	13
48.5	–	19.5	–	–	Anthony Giddens	13
48.5	34.5	–	–	–	Wayne Hall	13
48.5	–	–	–	–	L. John Horwood	13
48.5	–	–	–	–	Jody Miller	13
48.5	50	–	–	–	Tim Newburn	13

[a]Editor, 1998–2005

These articles contained a total of 20,256 cited authors, of which 1,189 were self-citations and 619 were coauthor citations. The 19,067 eligible cited authors (an average of 79 cited authors per article) may be compared with 15,326 in 2001–2005 (71 per article), 10,023 in 1996–2000 (59 per article), 6,771 in 1991–1995 (47 per article), and 5,665 in 1986–1990 (44 per article). Overall, the number of cited authors per BJC article has increased by about 80 % over this time period.

Table 3.2 shows the 51 most-cited scholars in BJC in 2006–2010. The most-cited scholar, David Garland, was cited 122 times. He was a versatile author, with 26 different works cited in 17 different articles (7 % of all BJC articles). His most-cited work, *The Culture of Control* (Garland, 2001), was cited 46 times. The second most-cited author in BJC, J. Michael Hough, was cited only 69 times. The highest-ranked female scholars were Barbara Hudson (ranked 24.5) and Lucia Zedner (ranked 30.5).

Table 3.2 also shows the comparable rankings of these scholars in the 4 earlier time periods. John Braithwaite, a versatile author, was the most-cited scholar in 2001–2005, and his most-cited work in that time period was *Crime, Shame, and Reintegration* (Braithwaite, 1989). Ken Pease was the most-cited scholar in 1996–2000. His most-cited work then was *The Kirkholt Burglary Prevention Project* (Forrester, Chatterton, & Pease, 1988), which was only cited 6 times, so he was primarily a versatile author. Patricia M. Mayhew was the most-cited scholar in 1991–1995. Her most-cited works then were *The 1988 British Crime Survey* (Mayhew, Elliott, & Dowds, 1989) and *The British Crime Survey* (Hough & Mayhew, 1983), so she was mainly a specialized author. The second most-cited scholar in 1991–1995, J. Michael Hough, was also best known for his work on the British Crime Survey. Stanley Cohen was the most-cited scholar in 1986–1990. He was also a specialized author, and his most-cited work then was *Visions of Social Control* (Cohen, 1985).

Twenty-five of the most-cited scholars in 2006–2010 (49 %) had been ranked in the top 50 in 2001–2005, compared with 20 in 1996–2000 (39 %), 15 in 1991–1996

3.2 *British Journal of Criminology* (BJC)

Table 3.2 Most-cited scholars in *British Journal of Criminology*

Rank in 2006–2010	Rank in 2001–2005	Rank in 1996–2000	Rank in 1991–1995	Rank in 1986–1990	Name	Cites
1	3	9	26.5	14	David Garland	122
2	17.5	4	2	3.5	J. Michael Hough	69
3	26.5	11	17	24	Michel Foucault	68
4	1	8	10	19	John Braithwaite	65
5	5	–	44.5	–	Robert J. Sampson	61
6	34	23	–	–	Patrick O'Malley[a]	60
7.5	2	6	5.5	3.5	David P. Farrington	59
7.5	–	–	–	–	Nikolas S. Rose	59
9	40.5	20	–	–	Jonathan Simon	58
10	19	36.5	–	–	Richard V. Ericson	57
11	–	–	–	–	Ian Loader	51
12	–	–	–	–	Tom R. Tyler	50
13.5	–	–	–	–	Stephen Farrall	48
13.5	10	13.5	17	44.5	Tony Jefferson	48
15	23	–	–	–	J. Richard Sparks	47
17	10	2	5.5	9	Ronald V. Clarke	46
17	4	11	–	–	Clifford D. Shearing	46
17	7	17	3.5	2	Jock Young	46
19	6	28	12	1	Stanley Cohen	44
20	15	–	–	–	Richard T. Wright	42
21	23.5	13.5	8	6	Anthony E. Bottoms	40
22	12.5	48	–	–	Tim Newburn	39
23	26.5	–	–	–	Benjamin Bowling	38
24.5	–	–	–	–	Ulrich Beck	37
24.5	–	–	–	–	Barbara Hudson	37
26	–	–	–	–	Daniel S. Nagin	36
27.5	–	–	–	–	John H. Laub	35
27.5	10	3	26.5	38.5	Robert Reiner	35
30.5	–	–	–	–	Zygmunt Baumann	34
30.5	–	–	–	–	Emile Durkheim	34
30.5	–	–	–	–	Loic Wacquant	34
30.5	–	–	–	–	Lucia Zedner	34
34.5	–	–	–	–	Pierre Bourdieu	33
34.5	–	–	–	–	Julian V. Roberts	33
34.5	31.5	–	29	–	Lawrence W. Sherman	33
34.5	–	–	–	–	Stephen Tombs	33
37	–	30	–	–	Malcolm M. Feeley	31
38.5	34	5	–	–	Anthony Giddens	30
38.5	26.5	–	–	–	Michael Levi	30
40	–	–	–	–	Mark Warr	28
41.5	–	–	–	–	Bruce A. Jacobs	27
41.5	–	–	–	–	Shadd Maruna	27
45.5	–	32.5	–	–	David H. Bayley	26
45.5	–	–	–	–	Francis T. Cullen	26

(continued)

Table 3.2 (continued)

Rank in 2006–2010	Rank in 2001–2005	Rank in 1996–2000	Rank in 1991–1995	Rank in 1986–1990	Name	Cites
45.5	45.5	–	–	30	Stuart Hall	26
45.5	–	–	39	38.5	Howard Parker	26
45.5	–	–	–	–	Alex R. Piquero	26
45.5	40.5	24.5	17	–	Wesley G. Skogan	26
50	–	–	–	–	Erving Goffman	25
50	–	–	–	–	Kieran McEvoy	25
50	–	–	–	–	Coretta Phillips	25

[a] From Australia

(29 %), and 13 in 1986–1990 (25 %). Eleven scholars, including the top 4 in 2006–2010, were ranked in the top 50 in all 5 time periods; only 1 additional scholar was ranked in the top 50 in 4 of the 5 time periods. David P. Farrington was ranked in the top 7 or 8 scholars in all 5 time periods. Between 2001–2005 and 2006–2010, big advances were made by J. Michael Hough (from 17.5 to 2), Michel Foucault (from 26.5 to 3), the Australian Patrick O'Malley (from 34 to 6), and Jonathan Simon (from 40.5 to 9). The highest new entrants were Nikolas S. Rose (7.5), Ian Loader (11), Tom R. Tyler (12), and Stephen Farrall (13.5). Moving downwards in rank between 2001–2005 and 2006–2010 were Clifford D. Shearing (from 4 to 17), Jock Young (from 7 to 17), and Stanley Cohen (from 6 to 19). Ten of the 11 most-cited scholars in 2001–2005 survived to be in the 50 most-cited scholars in 2006–2010: all except Ken Pease (ranked 8 in 2001–2005).

3.3 *Canadian Journal of Criminology and Criminal Justice* (CJC)

In CJC in 2006–2010, 136 articles were published by a total of 263 authors, most of whom (87 %, or 230) were Canadian. This is not too surprising, because CJC primarily publishes articles with a Canadian focus. Most commonly, the non-Canadian authors were American (11) or British (9). Both the number of articles published and the number of authors increased from 2001 to 2005, when there were 124 articles and 228 authors.

These articles contained a total of 7,741 cited authors, of which 452 were self-citations and 366 were coauthor citations. The 7,289 eligible citations (an average of 54 cited authors per article) may be compared with 6,143 in 2001–2005 (46 per article), 4,469 in 2000–2005 (43 per article), 4,184 in 1991–1995 (34 per article), and 4,049 in 1986–1990 (30 per article). The number of cited authors per CJC article increased by 80 % over this time period.

Table 3.3 shows the most-cited scholars in CJC in 2006–2010: those ranked up to 50. There are 47 names on this list (up to 10 citations); 9 scholars with 9 citations each were each ranked over 50. The most-cited scholar, Julian V. Roberts, was cited 33 times. Roberts, who was editor of CJC from 1993 to 2004, was a versatile author, because he had 29 different works cited in 17 different articles (13 % of all CJC articles). Most of his works were cited only once, but 4 of his works were cited 2 times each; these were "The incarceration of aboriginal offenders" (Roberts & Melchers, 2003), "Rapport de recherché: concernant la condamnation à l'emprisonnement avec sursis au Canada" (Roberts & LaPrairie, 2000), "Living in the shadow of prison" (Roberts & Gabor, 2004), and "Empty promises" (Stenning & Roberts, 2001). The second most-cited scholar was Anthony N. Doob, with 32 citations. The highest-ranked female scholars were Kelly Hannah-Moffat (ranked 7.5) and Terrie E. Moffitt (ranked 15.5).

Table 3.3 also shows the comparable rankings of these scholars in CJC in the 4 earlier time periods. Julian V. Roberts was also the most-cited scholar in 2001–2005 and 1996–2000. His 3 most-cited works in 2001–2005 only had 2 citations each. They were *The Use of Victim Impact Statements in Sentencing* (Roberts, 2002), "The incarceration of aboriginal offenders" (Roberts & Melchers, 2003), and "Empty promises" (Stenning & Roberts, 2001). His most-cited work in 1996–2000 was "Public opinion, crime, and criminal justice" (Roberts, 1992), but it was only cited 6 times. Murray A. Straus was the most-cited scholar in 1991–1995, and his most-cited work was *Behind Closed Doors* (Straus, Gelles, & Steinmetz, 1980). However, more than half of his citations in CJC appeared in 1 article (Lenton, 1995), so he had a low prevalence. Anthony N. Doob was the most-cited scholar in 1986–1990, and his most-cited work during that time period was *Sentencing* (Doob & Roberts, 1983).

Only 16 of the most-cited scholars in 2006–2010 (34 %) had been ranked in the top 50 in 2001–2005, compared with 17 in 1996–2000 (36 %), 10 in 1991–1995 (21 %), and 9 in 1986–1990 (19 %). Five scholars were ranked in the top 50 in all 5 time periods: Julian V. Roberts, Anthony N. Doob, Don A. Andrews, Paul Gendreau, and Nicholas Bala. Anthony N. Doob was ranked in the top 3 scholars in all 5 time periods. Four additional scholars were ranked in the top 50 in 4 out of the 5 time periods. Between 2001–2005 and 2006–2010, big advances were made by Richard V. Ericson (from 12 to 3.5), Robert J. Sampson (from 16.5 to 6), and Kevin D. Haggerty (from 34 to 18). The highest new entrants were Michel Foucault (ranked 5) and Kelly Hannah-Moffat (ranked 7.5). Moving downwards in rank between 2001–2005 and 2006–2010 were James L. Bonta (from 2 to 13) and Paul Gendreau (from 4 to 24). Seven of the 10 most-cited scholars in 2001–2005 survived to be in the 50 most-cited scholars in 2006–2010: all except Travis Hirschi (ranked 5 in 2001–2005), Lawrence W. Sherman (8), and Michael R. Gottfredson (9.5).

Table 3.3 Most-cited scholars in *Canadian Journal of Criminology and Criminal Justice*

Rank in 2006–2010	Rank in 2001–2005	Rank in 1996–2000	Rank in 1991–1995	Rank in 1986–1990	Name	Cites
1	1	1	23	16	Julian V. Roberts[a]	33
2	3	2	2.5	1	Anthony N. Doob	32
3.5	12	4	44.5	–	Richard V. Ericson	30
3.5	6	40.5	31	–	David P. Farrington	30
5	–	–	–	–	Michel Foucault	29
6	16.5	20.5	–	–	Robert J. Sampson	28
7.5	–	–	–	–	Kelly Hannah-Moffat	26
7.5	–	12	–	–	Clifford D. Shearing	26
9	–	34	–	–	David Garland	25
10	7	6	13	9	Don A. Andrews	24
11	–	34	–	–	Patrick O'Malley[b]	23
12	–	40.5	–	–	Nikolas S. Rose	20
13	2	9.5	–	11	James L. Bonta	19
14	16.5	–	–	–	R. Karl Hanson	18
15.5	–	–	–	–	Ulrich Beck	17
15.5	23.5	–	–	–	Terrie E. Moffitt	17
18	34	–	–	–	Kevin D. Haggerty	16
18	–	3	–	–	Robert D. Hare	16
18	–	–	–	–	John H. Laub	16
20.5	14	–	–	–	Peter J. Carrington[c]	15
20.5	12	7.5	–	4.5	Francis T. Cullen	15
24	–	–	31	22	Alfred Blumstein	14
24	–	–	–	–	Pierre Bourdieu	14
24	4	15	37.5	2	Paul Gendreau	14
24	9.5	–	–	–	Phillip C. Stenning	14
24	–	–	–	–	Scot Wortley	14
28	–	–	37.5	–	Rolf Loeber	13
28	–	–	–	–	Jennifer L. Schulenberg	13
28	–	–	–	–	Margaret Shaw	13
31	–	–	–	–	Carla Cesaroni	12
31	–	–	–	–	J. Michael Hough	12
31	–	–	–	–	George Pavlich	12
34.5	46.5	24	7	47.5	Nicholas Bala	11
34.5	–	–	–	–	Stanley Cohen	11
34.5	–	–	–	–	Alex R. Piquero	11
34.5	–	–	–	–	Tom R. Tyler	11
42	–	–	–	–	Zygmunt Bauman	10
42	–	–	–	–	Jacqueline Cohen	10
42	–	–	–	–	Timothy J. Hartnagel	10
42	–	–	–	–	Robert B. Kennedy	10
42	–	34	18.5	–	Carol LaPrairie	10

(continued)

Table 3.3 (continued)

Rank in 2006–2010	Rank in 2001–2005	Rank in 1996–2000	Rank in 1991–1995	Rank in 1986–1990	Name	Cites
42	–	29	–	22	Vernon L. Quinsey	10
42	–	–	–	–	Ralph B. Taylor	10
42	–	–	–	–	Mark S. Umbreit	10
42	–	–	–	–	Mark Warr	10
42	–	–	–	–	David B. Wexler	10
42	23.5	–	–	–	Ivan Zinger	10

[a] Editor, 1993–2004
[b] From Australia
[c] Editor, 2005 to present

3.4 *Criminology* (CRIM)

In CRIM in 2006–2010, 168 articles were published by a total of 413 individual authors, 90 % of whom (373) were American. The non-American authors were most commonly from Canada (11), the Netherlands (9), and the United Kingdom (7). While the number of articles published decreased (from 184 in 2001–2005), the number of authors hardly changed (from 417 in 2001–2005).

These articles contained a total of 21,969 cited authors, of which 1,110 were self-citations and 996 were coauthor citations. The 20,859 eligible cited authors (an average of 124 cited authors per article) may be compared with 19,936 in 2001–2005 (108 per article), 15,583 in 1996–2000 (91 per article), 10,650 in 1991–1995 (81 per article), and 11,405 in 1986–1990 (68 per article). Therefore, the number of cited authors per CRIM article increased by about 82 % over this time period.

Table 3.4 shows the most-cited scholars in CRIM in 2006–2010 (51 scholars with ranks up to 49.5). The most-cited scholar, Robert J. Sampson, was cited 363 times. His most-cited work in CRIM was *Crime in the Making* (Sampson & Laub, 1993), which was cited 33 times. In total, Sampson was cited in 105 different articles (63 % of all CRIM articles). He had a very high prevalence of citations as well as a high frequency, and his citations showed both specialization (1 very highly cited work) and versatility (78 different works cited).

Table 3.4 also shows the comparable rankings of these scholars in CRIM in the 4 earlier time periods. Sampson was also the most-cited scholar in 2001–2005 and 1996–2000, with *Crime in the Making* (Sampson & Laub, 1993) still his most-cited work. Travis Hirschi was the most-cited scholar in both 1991–1995 and 1986–1990, and his most-cited works were *A General Theory of Crime* (Gottfredson & Hirschi, 1990) in 1991–1995 and *Causes of Delinquency* (Hirschi, 1969) in 1986–1990. The highest-ranked female scholars in 2006–2010 were Terrie E. Moffitt (8.5) and Cassia C. Spohn (37.5).

Table 3.4 Most-cited scholars in *Criminology*

Rank in 2006–2010	Rank in 2001–2005	Rank in 1996–2000	Rank in 1991–1995	Rank in 1986–1990	Name	Cites
1	1	1	7	26	Robert J. Sampson	363
2	3	12	23.5	–	John H. Laub	147
3	10	37.5	–	–	Stephen W. Raudenbush	131
4	6	2	1	1	Travis Hirschi	125
5	24	–	45	–	Francis T. Cullen	116
6	5	11	20	–	Daniel S. Nagin	111
7	4	27	9.5	–	Raymond Paternoster[a]	101
8.5	2	20	–	–	Terrie E. Moffitt	97
8.5	7	–	–	–	Alex R. Piquero	97
10	11	3	2	9	Michael R. Gottfredson	95
11	8	5	3	2.5	David P. Farrington	91
12	9	14.5	–	42	Darrell J. Steffensmeier	86
13	13	4	16.5	–	Robert J. Bursik[b]	85
14	19.5	13	–	27	Steven F. Messner	82
15	12	20	5	6	Alfred Blumstein	77
16.5	21	6.5	13	–	Harold G. Grasmick	73
16.5	15	18	34.5	–	Kenneth C. Land	73
18	24	8	11.5	7	John L. Hagan	70
19	30	–	–	–	D. Wayne Osgood	67
20	30	–	–	–	Robert Brame	66
21.5	–	–	–	–	Shawn D. Bushway	64
21.5	14	–	–	–	Avshalom Caspi	64
23	17	24.5	45	–	William J. Wilson	62
24.5	16	28	–	–	Robert Agnew	61
24.5	–	–	–	–	Jeffrey D. Morenoff	61
26.5	26	16.5	14	22	Lawrence E. Cohen	58
26.5	41	9	8	20	Charles R. Tittle[c]	58
28	34	–	–	–.	Richard Rosenfeld	57
29	–	46	36.5	49.5	Marcus Felson	56
31	–	40	–	–	Lawrence W. Sherman	55
31	34	–	–	–	Jeffrey T. Ulmer	55
31	34	46	–	–	Mark Warr	55
33.5	27	34.5	–	–	Allen E. Liska	53
33.5	–	46	–	–	Ralph B. Taylor	53
35.5	–	–	41.5	–	Ronald V. Clarke	51
35.5	22	6.5	4	4	Delbert S. Elliott	51
37.5	49	20	15	15.5	Ronald L. Akers	48
37.5	46	–	–	–	Cassia C. Spohn	48
40	25	–	–	–	John H. Kramer	47
40	30	–	–	–	Janet L. Lauritsen	47

(continued)

3.5 Most-Cited Scholars in All Four Journals

Table 3.4 (continued)

Rank in 2006–2010	Rank in 2001–2005	Rank in 1996–2000	Rank in 1991–1995	Rank in 1986–1990	Name	Cites
40	–	–	–	–	David L. Weisburd	47
42.5	36.5	10	9.5	21	David Huizinga	46
42.5	–	–	–	–	Richard T. Wright	46
44	–	–	–	–	Anthony S. Bryk	44
45	41	24.5	20	14	Marvin D. Krohn	43
46.5	46	–	–	–	Elijah Anderson	42
46.5	48	–	–	–	Felton E. Earls	42
49.5	–	–	–	–	Celeste A. Albonetti	41
49.5	–	–	34.5	–	Theodore Chiricos	41
49.5	46	–	–	–	Ruth D. Peterson	41
49.5	–	–	–	–	Travis C. Pratt	41

[a]Editor, 2004–2005
[b]Editor, 1998–2003
[c]Editor, 1992–1997

Remarkably, 39 of the most-cited scholars in 2005–2010 (76 %) had been ranked in the top 50 in 2001–2005. Every 1 of the 20 most-cited authors in 2006–2010 was among the 50 most-cited authors in 2001–2005. In general, there is more stability over time in rankings of journals with larger numbers of citations (like CRIM) than in rankings of journals with smaller numbers of citations (like CJC), although changes in editors can cause changes in the types of articles published and hence changes in cited authors. Twenty-nine of the most-cited scholars in 2006–2010 (57 %) had been ranked in the top 50 in 1996–2000, compared with 23 in 1991–1995 (45 %) and 15 in 1986–1990 (29 %). Twelve scholars were ranked in the top 50 in all 5 time periods, and an additional 10 were ranked in the top 50 in 4 out of the 5 time periods. Travis Hirschi was ranked in the top 6 scholars in all time periods.

Between 2001–2005 and 2006–2010, big advances were made by Stephen W. Raudenbush (from 10 to 3) and Francis T. Cullen (from 24 to 5). The highest new entrants were Shawn D. Bushway (21.5) and Jeffrey D. Morenoff (24.5). Moving downwards in rank between 2001–2005 and 2006–2010 were Delbert S. Elliott (from 22 to 35.5) and John H. Kramer (from 25 to 40). All of the 17 most-cited scholars in 2001–2005 survived to be in the 50 most-cited scholars in 2006–2010; the highest-ranked scholars in 2001–2005 who did not survive were Paul Mazerolle (18) and Rolf Loeber (19.5).

3.5 Most-Cited Scholars in All Four Journals

In order to produce a combined measure of influence based on all 4 journals, each cited scholar was given a score of 51 minus his or her rank on citations in each journal. Thus, the most-cited scholar in each journal was given a score of 50, and all scholars ranked outside the top 50 in a journal were scored 0. The scores on all 4 journals were then added for each scholar, yielding a total score out of a theoretical maximum of 200. This measure gives equal weight to all 4 journals. If all citations had merely been added, scholars who were highly cited in journals with a relatively high number of citations (e.g., CRIM) would have predominated.

Table 3.5 shows the 30 most-cited scholars on this combined measure. All except Anthony N. Doob were highly cited in at least 2 of the 4 journals. Only 5 scholars were highly cited in all 4 journals: Robert J. Sampson, David P. Farrington, John H. Laub, Francis T. Cullen, and Alex R. Piquero. Eleven additional scholars were among the 50 most-cited scholars in 3 of the 4 journals. The only female scholar in this list is Terrie E. Moffitt (ranked 6.5).

Of the 30 most-cited scholars, 24 were highly cited in ANZ, 20 were highly cited in BJC and CJC, but only 16 were highly cited in CRIM. The rankings of scholars were most concordant between ANZ and CRIM and between BJC and CJC, and least concordant between BJC and CRIM and between CJC and CRIM. All 16 of the highly cited scholars in CRIM were also highly cited in ANZ, while 6 scholars were not highly cited in either, giving a concordance of 22 out of 30. Of the 20 scholars who were highly cited in BJC, 16 were also highly cited in CJC, and vice versa, while 6 scholars were not highly cited in either, giving the same concordance of 22 out of 30. In contrast, only 7 scholars out of 20 who were highly cited in CJC were highly cited in CRIM (total concordance = 8) and only 8 scholars out of 20 who were highly cited in BJC were highly cited in CRIM (total concordance = 10). Therefore, the 4 journals could be grouped into 2 concordant pairs with regard to the most-cited scholars.

Table 3.5 also shows the comparable rankings of these scholars in the 4 earlier time periods (up to rank 50). Twenty-five of the 30 most-cited scholars in 2006–2010 (83 %) were highly cited in 2001–2005, compared with 19 in 1996–2000 (63 %), 16 in 1991–1995 (53 %), and 10 in 1986–1990 (33 %). The most-cited scholar in 2006–2010, Robert J. Sampson, did not appear in the table in 1986–1990 but then advanced steadily from 18 in 1991–1995 to 10 in 1996–2000, 2 in 2001–2005, and 1 in 2006–2010. His citation career increased as he became more influential, being appointed to a Professorship at Harvard University in 2003. David P. Farrington was among the top 3 scholars in all 5 time periods. Only 7 of the 30 most-cited scholars in 2006–2010 were among the 50 most-cited in all 5 time periods (David P. Farrington, John Braithwaite, Travis Hirschi, Ronald V. Clarke, Michael R. Gottfredson, Stanley Cohen, and Anthony N. Doob); an additional 8 were among the 50 most-cited scholars in 4 of the 5 time periods.

Between 2001–2005 and 2006–2010, big advances were made by Daniel S. Nagin (from 29.5 to 5) and Alex R. Piquero (from 36.5 to 8). The highest new entrants were Tom R. Tyler (12) and Nikolas S. Rose (19). Moving in the opposite direction were Travis Hirschi (from 3 to 17) and Michael R. Gottfredson (from 4 to 23.5). Nine of the top 10 scholars in 2001–2005 remained in the table in 2006–2010: all except Jock Young (ranked 9 in 2001–2005).

Table 3.6 shows the most-cited works of the 10 most-cited scholars in 2006–2010. These were mostly books rather than journal articles. David Garland was the

3.5 Most-Cited Scholars in All Four Journals

Table 3.5 Most-cited scholars in four international journals

Rank in 2006–2010	Rank in 2001–2005	Rank in 1996–2000	Rank in 1991–1995	Rank in 1986–1990	Name	Score in ANZ	Score in BJC	Score in CJC	Score in CRIM	Total score
1	2	10	18	–	Robert J. Sampson	50	46	45	50	191
2	1	3	2	3	David P. Farrington	49	43.5	47.5	40	180
3	12	45	–	–	John H. Laub	44.5	23.5	33	49	150
4	8	2	14	–	David Garland	29	50	42	0	121
5	29.5	41	–	–	Daniel S. Nagin	46.5	25	0	45	116.5
6.5	16	34	–	29	Francis T. Cullen	32	5.5	30.5	46	114
6.5	6	–	–	–	Terrie E. Moffitt	36	0	35.5	42.5	114
8	36.5	–	–	–	Alex R. Piquero	44.5	5.5	16.5	42.5	109
9	23	22	–	–	Julian V. Roberts	37	16.5	50	0	103.5
10	10	11.5	–	–	Clifford D. Shearing	25	34.5	43.5	0	103
11	17	–	4	2	Alfred Blumstein	39	0	27	36	102
12	–	–	–	–	Tom R. Tyler	41	39	16.5	0	96.5
13	7	1	5	11	John Braithwaite	48	47	0	0	95
14	19.5	9	12	–	Michel Foucault	0	48	46	0	94
15	27	21	39.5	–	Raymond Paternoster	46.5	0	0	44	90.5
16	14	4	–	–	Richard V. Ericson	0	41	47.5	0	88.5
17	3	8	1	7	Travis Hirschi	39	0	0	47	86
18	21	6	30	–	Patrick O'Malley	0	45	40	0	85
19	–	–	–	–	Nikolas S. Rose	0	43.5	39	0	82.5
20	–	20	21.5	27	J. Michael Hough	11	49	20	0	80
21	11	25.5	16.5	8	Ronald V. Clarke	25	34.5	0	15.5	75
22	41.5	–	–	–	Darrell J. Steffensmeier	25	0	0	39	64
23.5	4	11.5	3	20	Michael R. Gottfredson	21	0	0	41	62
23.5	–	–	–	–	Ulrich Beck	0	26.5	35.5	0	62

(continued)

Table 3.5 (continued)

Rank in 2006–2010	Rank in 2001–2005	Rank in 1996–2000	Rank in 1991–1995	Rank in 1986–1990	Name	Score in ANZ	Score in BJC	Score in CJC	Score in CRIM	Total score
25	5	–	15	–	Lawrence W. Sherman	25	16.5	0	20	61.5
26	–	–	–	–	Robert Brame	29	0	0	31	60
27	45	–	–	–	Stephen W. Raudenbush	11	0	0	48	59
28	22	–	28	–	Rolf Loeber	29	0	23	0	52
29	29.5	17	8	5	Stanley Cohen	2	32	16.5	0	50.5
30	25	25.5	24	22.5	Anthony N. Doob	0	0	49	0	49

3.5 Most-Cited Scholars in All Four Journals

Table 3.6 Most-cited works of the most-cited scholars

Rank	Author/work	Number of citations
1	Robert J. Sampson (93 different works cited)	
	Sampson, R. J., & Laub, J. H. (1993). *Crime in the making.* Cambridge, MA: Harvard University Press.	51
	Sampson, R. J., Raudenbush, S. W., & Earls F. (1997). Neighborhoods and violent crime: A multilevel study of collective efficacy. *Science, 277,* 918–924.	45
2	David P. Farrington (122 different works cited)	
	Piquero, A. R., Farrington, D. P., & Blumstein, A. (2003). The criminal career paradigm. In M. Tonry (Ed.), *Crime and justice* (vol. 30, pp. 359–506). Chicago: University of Chicago Press.	16
	Piquero, A. R., Farrington, D. P., & Blumstein, A. (2007). *Key issues in criminal career research.* Cambridge, UK: Cambridge University Press.	9
3	John H. Laub (48 different works cited)	
	Sampson, R. J., & Laub, J. H. (1993). *Crime in the making.* Cambridge, MA: Harvard University Press.	50
	Laub J. H., & Sampson R. J. (2003). *Shared beginnings, divergent lives.* Cambridge, MA: Harvard University Press.	34
4	David Garland (33 different works cited)	
	Garland, D. (2001). *The culture of control.* Oxford, UK: Oxford University Press.	73
	Garland, D. (1990). *Punishment and modern society.* Oxford, UK: Clarendon Press.	18
5	Daniel S. Nagin (61 different works cited)	
	Nagin, D. S. (2005). *Group-based modeling of development.* Cambridge, MA: Harvard University Press.	12
	Three works with 10 cites each	
6.5	Francis T. Cullen (98 different works cited)	
	Pratt, T. C. & Cullen, F. T. (2000). The empirical status of Gottfredson and Hirschi's general theory of crime: A meta-analysis. *Criminology, 38,* 931–964.	11
	Pratt, T. C., & Cullen, F. T. (2005). Assessing macro-level predictors and theories of crime: A meta-analysis. In M. Tonry (Ed.) *Crime and justice* (vol. 32, pp. 373–450). Chicago: University of Chicago Press.	9
6.5	Terrie E. Moffitt (50 different works cited)	
	Moffitt, T. E. (1993). Adolescence-limited and life-course persistent antisocial behavior: A developmental taxonomy. *Psychological Review, 100,* 674–701.	33
	Moffitt, T. E., Caspi, A., Rutter, M., & Silva, P. A. (2001). *Sex differences in antisocial behaviour.* Cambridge, UK: Cambridge University Press.	10
8	Alex R. Piquero (70 different works cited)	
	Piquero, A. R., Farrington, D. P., & Blumstein, A. (2003). The criminal career paradigm. In M. Tonry (Ed.), *Crime and justice* (vol. 30, pp. 359–506). Chicago: University of Chicago Press.	12
	Piquero, A. R., Farrington, D. P., & Blumstein, A. (2007). *Key issues in criminal career research.* Cambridge, UK: Cambridge University Press.	8

(continued)

Table 3.6 (continued)

Rank	Author/work	Number of citations
9	Julian V. Roberts (58 different works cited)	
	Roberts, J. V., Stalans, L. J., Indermaur, D., & Hough, J. M. (2003). *Penal populism and public opinion.* New York: Oxford University Press.	9
	Roberts, J. V. & Stalans. L. J. (1997). *Public opinion, crime, and criminal justice.* Boulder, CO: Westview Press.	5
	Roberts, J. V., & Hough, J. M. (2005). *Understanding public attitudes to criminal justice.* New York: Open University Press.	5
10	Clifford D. Shearing (42 different works cited)	
	Johnston, L., & Shearing, C. D. (2003). *Governing security.* New York: Routledge.	13
	Bayley, D., & Shearing, C. D. (2001). *The new structure of policing.* Washington, DC: U.S. National Institute of Justice.	7

most specialized scholar, as he had relatively few works cited and 1 very highly cited work (*The Culture of Control*). David P. Farrington was the most versatile scholar, as he had relatively many works cited and no very highly cited work. Robert J. Sampson was both specialized and versatile, since he had many different works cited but also 2 highly cited works.

3.6 Conclusion

The main strengths of this research lie in the extensive checking, informed by knowledge about the field of criminology and of criminologists, in an effort to minimize the many errors that appear in mechanical analyses of citations (e.g., through the use of SSCI). For example, much effort was devoted to distinguishing between different individuals with the same name, such as the Australian (sometime Canadian-based) Patrick O'Malley and the American Patrick M. O'Malley. Unlike SSCI, all self-citations were excluded. Another important strength of this research is the collection of comparable citation data from major international criminological journals over a 25-year period. This makes it possible to identify the increasing scholarly influence of younger scholars such as Robert J. Sampson and the decreasing influence of older scholars such as Travis Hirschi.

This research is based on citations in only a small number of mainstream CCJ journals in the English-speaking world (although Canada is bilingual). This is both a strength and a weakness. The selected journals are all prestigious criminology journals, allowing a research focus on citations in these specific journals. If a more generic source of citation data, such as SSCI, had been used, citations from a wide variety of journals that either are less prestigious or have little or nothing to do with

3.6 Conclusion

criminology would have been included. However, the research is limited to journals that were being published in 1986, when this analysis of citations began, and thus it is not possible to include more recent journals. For example, if the research was beginning today, the *European Journal of Criminology* would most likely have been included.

The small number of journals examined also means that this research probably underestimates the influence of scholars whose research focuses on very narrow specialities, or who publish primarily in other disciplines, and who may not be highly cited in these more mainstream CCJ journals. While some criminologists may be very influential within their limited areas of specialization, they may not be widely cited in the more mainstream CCJ journals.

The most-cited scholars will vary depending on the journals (or other sources) analyzed and the time period. CJC, BJC, and ANZ include criminal justice topics as well as (or more than) criminology topics, whereas CRIM focuses on criminology and includes only a limited number of articles on criminal justice topics. Arguably, American criminology/criminal justice research would be better represented by analyzing both CRIM and *Justice Quarterly*, as indeed Cohn and Farrington (1994b) have done. However, the aim of the present chapter was to analyze citations in the 1 major journal in each of the 4 English-speaking countries, and CRIM is undoubtedly the major criminological journal in the United States.

In 2006–2010, the most-cited scholars in these 4 journals were Robert J. Sampson in ANZ and CRIM, David Garland in BJC, and Julian V. Roberts in CJC. In all 4 journals combined, the most-cited scholars were Robert J. Sampson, David P. Farrington, John H. Laub, David Garland, and Daniel S. Nagin. The most-cited works of the most-cited authors show that some scholars were specialized, because they had a large number of citations of 1 or 2 seminal works, usually books and often theoretical in nature. Other scholars were versatile, because they had many different works cited a few times each. Therefore, there are 2 different ways in which scholarly influence operates in criminology and criminal justice.

Over time, the average number of cited authors per article has tended to increase. This may reflect either the increasing volume of criminological literature over time or the increasing ease of accessing it. Twenty-five years ago, it was much more difficult for scholars to obtain and read source works, as they had to obtain printed copies of journal articles from their university library or request them through interlibrary loan. Today, more and more journals are available online in a full-text format and can be accessed anywhere, as long as a scholar has Internet access. It might be expected that, in light of the increasing accessibility of journal articles, scholars will cite more articles than books in the future. However, in these analyses, books were still the most-cited works of the most-cited scholars.

To a considerable extent, all 4 journals tended to be parochial, with the majority of published articles written by scholars from their own countries. BJC was the most international and least parochial of the four, with only 50 % of published articles written by scholars from the United Kingdom. CJC and CRIM were the most parochial; approximately 90 % of the published articles in each journal were written by scholars from the home country. Thus, the field of criminology does not appear to truly reflect the increasing globalization of the world as a whole. Given the diminution of national boundaries, the ever-increasing integration of formerly distinct communities, and the growing internationalization of society, it is clear that criminology ideally needs to follow social trends and become more global, with increasing communication and collaboration among criminologists from different countries, and with a greater emphasis on cross-national collaborative studies designed to compare and contrast theories and findings in different countries.

Chapter 4
Most-Cited Scholars in Six American Criminology and Criminal Justice Journals

This chapter examines the most-cited scholars in 2006–2010 in 3 major American criminology journals (*Criminology*—CRIM, *Journal of Quantitative Criminology*—JQC, *Journal of Research in Crime and Delinquency*—JRCD) and 3 major American criminal justice journals (*Justice Quarterly*—JQ, *Journal of Criminal Justice*—JCJ, *Criminal Justice and Behavior*—CJB). The most-cited works of the most-cited scholars are also listed. Comparisons are made with 4 earlier time periods (1986–1990, 1991–1995, 1996–2000, and 2001–2005) so that changes in the influence and prestige of scholars during the past 25 years can be documented. As we listed the most-cited scholars in CRIM in Chapter 3, we begin with JQC.

4.1 *Journal of Quantitative Criminology* (JQC)

In JQC in 2006–2010, 103 articles were published by a total of 232 authors, 86 % of whom (199) were American. The non-American authors were most commonly from the Netherlands (16) and the United Kingdom (12). These articles contained a total of 11,571 cited authors, of which 677 were self-citations and 602 were coauthor citations. The 10,894 eligible cited authors (an average of 106 per article) may be compared with 6,977 in 2001–2005 (78 per article), 7,395 in 1996–2000 (79 per article), 5,839 in 1991–1995 (69 per article), and 4,708 in 1986–1990 (47 per article), showing that the number of cited authors per article in JQC more than doubled over this time period. Between 2001–2005 and 2006–2010, there was only a small increase in the number of articles published (from 90 to 103), but there was a big increase in the number of cited authors per article (from 78 to 106).

Table 4.1 shows 47 scholars ranked up to 50 in JQC in 2006–2010. The most-cited scholar, Robert J. Sampson, was cited 182 times. He was a versatile author, since he had 59 different works cited in 59 different articles (57 % of all JQC articles). His most-cited work, *Crime in the Making* (Sampson & Laub, 1993) was

Table 4.1 Most-cited scholars in *Journal of Quantitative Criminology*

Rank in 2006–2010	Rank in 2001–2005	Rank in 1996–2000	Rank in 1991–1995	Rank in 1986–1990	Name	Cites
1	2.5	3	6	–	Robert J. Sampson	182
2	1	4.5	12.5	–	Daniel S. Nagin	143
3	13	–	–	–	Alex R. Piquero[a]	98
4	6	1	2	9.5	David P. Farrington	97
5	10.5	12	18	–	John H. Laub[b]	85
6	7	2	3	2	Alfred Blumstein	84
7	8	40	44.5	–	Raymond Paternoster	80
8	33.5	6	4	5.5	Jacqueline Cohen	69
9	20.5	–	–	–	Stephen W. Raudenbush	67
10	33.5	–	–	–	Robert Brame	64
11	2.5	4.5	1	8	Travis Hirschi	62
12	4	7.5	21	49	Kenneth C. Land	61
13	5	7.5	5	4	Michael R. Gottfredson	54
14	9	–	–	–	Terrie E. Moffitt	52
15	37.5	–	–	–	D. Wayne Osgood	51
16.5	–	–	44.5	11.5	Marcus Felson	44
16.5	–	–	–	–	David L. Weisburd	44
18	–	–	–	–	Shawn D. Bushway	43
19	27	–	–	–	Robert J. Bursik	42
20	22.5	–	–	–	Francis T. Cullen	39
21.5	–	–	–	–	Patricia L. Brantingham	37
21.5	15	9	28.5	–	Rolf Loeber	37
23.5	–	–	–	–	Paul J. Brantingham	36
23.5	41.5	16	12.5	3	Lawrence E. Cohen	36
25	33.5	27.5	35	–	Lawrence W. Sherman	34
26	–	–	39	–	Steven F. Messner	33
27	–	–	–	–	Richard Rosenfeld	32
28.5	30	–	–	–	Donald B. Rubin	30
28.5	–	–	–	–	Jeffrey T. Ulmer	30
30	–	–	–	–	Harold G. Grasmick	29
33	–	–	–	–	John E. Eck	28
33	–	–	–	–	Steven D. Levitt	28
33	–	–	–	–	Jeffrey D. Morenoff	28
33	18	36	18	–	Darrell J. Steffensmeier	28
33	37.5	–	–	–	Richard E. Tremblay	28
37.5	10.5	14	7	25	Delbert S. Elliott	27
37.5	–	–	–	–	Paul R. Rosenbaum	27
37.5	–	–	–	–	Ralph B. Taylor	27
37.5	–	–	–	–	Mark Warr	27

(continued)

Table 4.1 (continued)

Rank in 2006–2010	Rank in 2001–2005	Rank in 1996–2000	Rank in 1991–1995	Rank in 1986–1990	Name	Cites
40	–	20	–	–	Ken Pease	26
42.5	16	–	–	–	Avshalom Caspi	25
42.5	45.5	50.5	–	–	Terance D. Miethe	25
42.5	50	–	–	–	Cassia C. Spohn	25
42.5	27	27.5	15.5	–	Terence P. Thornberry	25
46	–	–	–	–	Anne M. Piehl	24
46	–	–	–	–	Michael H. Tonry	24
46	–	20	15.5	1	Marvin E. Wolfgang	24

[a]Editor, 2009–2013
[b]Editor, 1992–1996

cited 17 times. The second most-cited scholar, Daniel S. Nagin, was cited 143 times. The highest-ranked female scholars were Jacqueline Cohen ranked 8 and Terrie E. Moffitt (14).

Table 4.1 also shows the comparable rankings of these scholars in JQC in the 4 earlier time periods. Nagin was the most-cited author in 2001–2005. His most-cited works, each with 7 citations, were "A comparison of Poisson, negative binomial, and semiparametric mixed Poisson regression models with empirical applications to criminal careers research" (Land, McCall, & Nagin, 1996), "Age, criminal careers, and population heterogeneity" (Nagin & Land, 1993) and "Trajectories of change in criminal offending" (Laub, Nagin, & Sampson, 1998). David P. Farrington was the most-cited scholar in 1996–2000, and his most-cited work then was "The stability of criminal potential from childhood to adulthood" (Nagin & Farrington, 1992). Travis Hirschi was the most-cited scholar in 1991–1995, and his most-cited work then was *Causes of Delinquency* (Hirschi, 1969). Marvin E. Wolfgang was the most-cited scholar in 1986–1990, and his most-cited work then was *Delinquency in a Birth Cohort* (Wolfgang, Figlio, & Sellin, 1972). Twenty-eight of these 47 scholars (60 %) had been ranked in the top 50 in 2001–2005, 19 (40 %) in 1996–2000 and 1991–1995, and 10 (21 %) in 1986–1990. Only 5 scholars were ranked in the top 50 in all 5 time periods; 9 additional scholars were ranked in the top 50 in 4 of the 5 time periods. Alfred Blumstein, David P. Farrington, Michael R. Gottfredson, and Travis Hirschi were among the most-cited 13 scholars in all 5 time periods.

Between 2001–2005 and 2006–2010, big advances were made by Alex R. Piquero (from 13 to 3), Jacqueline Cohen (from 33.5 to 8), Stephen W. Raudenbush (from 20.5 to 9), and Robert Brame (from 33.5 to 10). The highest new entrants were David L. Weisburd (16.5) and Shawn D. Bushway (18). Moving downwards in rank between 2001–2005 and 2006–2010 were Delbert S. Elliott (from 10.5 to 37.5) and Avshalom Caspi (from 16 to 42.5). All of the 11 most-cited scholars in 2001–2005 survived to be in the 47 most-cited scholars in 2006–2010; the highest-ranked scholars who did not survive were David Cantor (ranked 12 in 2001–2005) and Robert Agnew (14).

4.2 *Journal of Research in Crime and Delinquency* (JRCD)

In JRCD in 2006–2010, 89 articles were published by a total of 221 authors, 90 % of whom (198) were American. The non-American authors were most commonly from the Netherlands (7), the United Kingdom (3), and Australia (3). These articles contained a total of 11,411 cited authors, of which 556 were self-citations and 577 were coauthor citations. The 10,855 eligible cited authors (an average of 122 per article) may be compared with 8,944 in 2001–2005 (108 per article), 8,590 in 1996–2000 (94 per article), 7,121 in 1991–1995 (68 per article), and 5,422 in 1986–1990 (67 per article), so that the number of cited authors per article in JRCD increased by 82 % over this time period.

Table 4.2 shows the most-cited scholars in JRCD in 2006–2010. The most-cited scholar, Robert J. Sampson, was cited 177 times. His most-cited work in JRCD, as in JQC, was *Crime in the Making* (Sampson & Laub, 1993), which was cited 18 times. In total, Sampson had 53 different works cited in 57 different articles (64 % of all JRCD articles). The second most-cited scholar, Terrie E. Moffitt, was also the most highly-cited female scholar.

Table 4.2 also shows the comparable rankings of these scholars in JRCD in the 4 earlier time periods. Sampson was also the most-cited scholar in 2001–2005 and 1996–2000, and his most-cited work in both time periods was *Crime in the Making* (Sampson & Laub, 1993). Travis Hirschi was the most-cited scholar in 1991–1995 and 1986–1990. His most-cited work in both time periods was *Causes of Delinquency* (Hirschi, 1969), although this was closely followed by *A General Theory of Crime* (Gottfredson & Hirschi, 1990) in 1991–1995. Only Travis Hirschi and Michael R. Gottfredson were among the most-cited ten scholars in all 5 time periods. Thirty-five of these 47 scholars (74 %) had been ranked in the top 50 in 2001–2005, 30 (64 %) in 1996–2000, 23 (49 %) in 1991–1995, and 14 (30 %) in 1986–1990. Thirteen scholars were ranked in the top 50 in all 5 time periods while 9 additional scholars were ranked in the top 50 in 4 of the 5 time periods.

Between 2001–2005 and 2006–2010, big advances were made by Alex R. Piquero (from 30.5 to 7), D. Wayne Osgood (from 44 to 14), and Avshalom Caspi (from 30.5 to 15.5). The highest new entrants were Travis C. Pratt (23), Dana L. Haynie (35), and John P. Wright (35). Moving downwards in rank between 2001–2005 and 2006–2010 were Delbert S. Elliott (from 9 to 25.5) and Robert J. Bursik (from 7 to 35). All of the 13 most-cited scholars in 2001–2005 survived to be in the 47 most-cited scholars in 2006–2010; the highest-ranked scholars who did not survive were Charles R. Tittle (ranked 14 in 2001–2005) and Ralph B. Taylor (16).

4.2 Journal of Research in Crime and Delinquency (JRCD)

Table 4.2 Most-cited scholars in *Journal of Research in Crime and Delinquency*

Rank in 2006–2010	Rank in 2001–2005	Rank in 1996–2000	Rank in 1991–1995	Rank in 1986–1990	Name	Cites
1	1	1	6	20.5	Robert J. Sampson	177
2	5	24.5	–	–	Terrie E. Moffitt	95
3	4	8	5	–	David P. Farrington	86
4.5	9	49.5	35	–	Francis T. Cullen	84
4.5	2	2	1	1	Travis Hirschi	84
6	12	12	–	–	John H. Laub	78
7	30.5	–	–	–	Alex R. Piquero	77
8	9	24.5	35	–	Daniel S. Nagin	69
9	3	3	4	6	Michael R. Gottfredson	67
10	6	14	7	14	Raymond Paternoster	64
11	13	28.5	39	–	Rolf Loeber	63
12	11	5.5	–	–	Robert Agnew	55
13	19	–	–	–	Stephen W. Raudenbush	50
14	44	–	–	–	D. Wayne Osgood	48
15.5	23.5	24.5	15	18	Alfred Blumstein	46
15.5	30.5	–	–	–	Avshalom Caspi	46
17	32	4	–	–	Terence P. Thornberry	45
18	36	–	–	–	Robert Brame	43
19	17.5	7	3	–	David Huizinga	42
20	21	28.5	31	–	Kenneth C. Land	41
21	–	40	–	–	Mark Warr	38
23	–	17	11	38.5	Marcus Felson	37
23	–	–	–	–	Travis C. Pratt	37
23	40.5	–	–	–	Darrell J. Steffensmeier	37
25.5	9	5.5	2	11.5	Delbert S. Elliott	36
25.5	40.5	–	–	–	Paul J. Mazerolle	36
27	23.5	10	20.5	11.5	Marvin D. Krohn	35
28.5	44	15.5	24	2	Michael J. Hindelang	34
28.5	48.5	24.5	–	–	Terance D. Miethe	34
30	44	10	13	29.5	Ronald L. Akers	33
31.5	36	20	8	4	Lawrence E. Cohen	32
31.5	–	36.5	–	–	Janet L. Lauritsen	32
35	7	13	9	–	Robert J. Bursik	31
35	15	18	19	34.5	Harold G. Grasmick	31
35	–	–	–	–	Dana L. Haynie	31
35	28.5	–	–	–	Phil A. Silva	31
35	–	–	–	–	John P. Wright	31
38	48.5	10	15	3	John L. Hagan	28

(continued)

Table 4.2 (continued)

Rank in 2006–2010	Rank in 2001–2005	Rank in 1996–2000	Rank in 1991–1995	Rank in 1986–1990	Name	Cites
39	26	19	45.5	–	Steven F. Messner	27
40.5	48.5	40	27	29.5	Jacqueline Cohen	26
40.5	–	–	–	–	Jeffrey D. Morenoff	26
42	–	–	–	–	Felton J. Earls	25
43.5	–	–	–	–	Peggy C. Giordano	23
43.5	–	36.5	–	–	Allen Liska	23
46	–	–	35	–	Ronald V. Clarke	22
46	–	–	–	–	Christopher J. Schreck	22
46	36	–	–	–	Magda Stouthamer-Loeber	22

4.3 Most-Cited Scholars in Three Criminology Journals

There was considerable agreement among the 3 criminology journals as to the most-cited scholars in 2006–2010. David P. Farrington, Travis Hirschi, John H. Laub, Daniel S. Nagin, Raymond Paternoster, Alex R. Piquero, and Robert J. Sampson were among the 11 most-cited scholars in all 3 journals. Of these, Farrington, Hirschi, Nagin, Paternoster, and Sampson were among the 9 most-cited scholars in all 3 journals in 2001–2005, and Sampson, Farrington, and Hirschi were among the 8 most-cited scholars in all 3 journals in 1996–2000.

In order to produce a combined measure of influence based on all 3 criminology journals, each cited author was given a score of 51 minus his or her rank on citations in each individual journal. Thus, the most-cited author in each journal was scored 50, and all authors ranked outside the top 50 in a journal were scored zero. The scores on all 3 journals were then added for each author, to yield a total score out of a theoretical maximum of 150. The purpose of this method is to ensure that equal weight is given to each journal. If we had simply added the total number of citations, then authors cited in journals with a relatively high number of citations (e.g., CRIM) would have dominated.

Table 4.3 shows the 30 most-cited scholars in the 3 American criminology journals according to this combined measure. All were ranked in the top 50 in at least 2 journals, and the top 22 scholars were ranked in the top 50 in all 3 journals. Robert J. Sampson was the most-cited scholar in all 3 journals, and the most-cited female scholar was Terrie E. Moffitt (8).

We also determined the most-cited works of the most-cited scholars in these 3 journals. For Robert J. Sampson, these were *Crime in the Making* (Sampson & Laub, 1993), with 68 citations, and "Neighborhoods and violent crime" (Sampson, Raudenbush, & Earls, 1997) with 58 citations. For John H. Laub, these were *Crime in the Making* (Sampson & Laub, 1993), with 66 citations, and *Shared Beginnings,*

4.3 Most-Cited Scholars in Three Criminology Journals

Table 4.3 Most-cited scholars in three American criminology journals

Rank in 2006–2010	Rank in 2001–2005	Rank in 1996–2000	Rank in 1991–1995	Rank in 1986–1990	Name	Score in CRIM	Score in JQC	Score in JRCD	Total
1	1	1	5	21	Robert J. Sampson	50	50	50	150
2	8	8	28	–	John H. Laub	49	46	45	140
3	3	9	17	–	Daniel S. Nagin	45	49	43	137
4	5.5	4	2	10	David P. Farrington	40	47	48	135
5	16	–	–	–	Alex R. Piquero	42.5	48	44	134.5
6	2	2	1	1	Travis Hirschi	47	40	46.5	133.5
7	5.5	24	14	30	Raymond Paternoster	44	44	41	129
8	4	28	–	–	Terrie E. Moffitt	42.5	37	49	128.5
9	15	–	–	–	Stephen W. Raudenbush	48	42	38	128
10	17	–	–	–	Francis T. Cullen	46	31	46.5	123.5
11	7	3	3	4	Michael R. Gottfredson	41	38	42	121
12	12	11	7	5	Alfred Blumstein	36	45	35.5	116.5
13.5	–	–	–	–	D. Wayne Osgood	32	36	37	105
13.5	28	–	–	–	Robert Brame	31	41	33	105
15	9	16	23	–	Kenneth C. Land	34	39	31	104
16	13	20	20	–	Robert J. Bursik	38	32	16	86
17	19	–	–	–	Darrell J. Steffensmeier	39	18	28	85
18	–	29	27	25	Marcus Felson	22	34.5	28	84.5
19	27	25	–	–	Steven F. Messner	37	25	12	74
20	18	–	–	–	Avshalom Caspi	29.5	8.5	35.5	73.5
21	23	22	21.5	–	Harold G. Grasmick	35	21	16	72
22	30	14.5	8	6	Lawrence E. Cohen	24.5	27.5	19.5	71.5
23	14	21	26	–	Rolf Loeber	0	29.5	40	69.5

(continued)

Table 4.3 (continued)

Rank in 2006–2010	Rank in 2001–2005	Rank in 1996–2000	Rank in 1991–1995	Rank in 1986–1990	Name	Score in CRIM	Score in JQC	Score in JRCD	Total
24	10	17	–	–	Robert Agnew	26.5	0	39	65.5
25	–	–	–	–	Mark Warr	20	13.5	30	63.5
26	–	–	–	–	Shawn D. Bushway	29.5	33	0	62.5
27	–	–	–	–	Jeffrey D. Morenoff	26.5	18	10.5	55
28	11	5	4	8	Delbert S. Elliott	15.5	13.5	25.5	54.5
29	–	23	9	9	Jacqueline Cohen	0	43	10.5	53.5
30	–	–	–	–	Richard Rosenfeld	23	24	0	47

Divergent Lives (Laub & Sampson, 2003), with 44 citations. Laub had slightly fewer citations for *Crime in the Making* because self-citations were not counted.

The most-cited works of Daniel S. Nagin were "Age, criminal careers, and population heterogeneity" (Nagin & Land, 1993), with 25 citations, and *Group-Based Modeling of Development* (Nagin, 2005), with 24 citations. The most-cited works of David P. Farrington were "The criminal career paradigm" (Piquero, Farrington, & Blumstein, 2003), with 26 citations, and "Age and crime" (Farrington, 1986), with 15 citations. The most-cited works of Alex R. Piquero were "The criminal career paradigm" (Piquero et al., 2003), with 15 citations, and "Using the correct statistical test for the equality of regression coefficients" (Paternoster, Brame, Mazerolle, & Piquero, 1998), with 14 citations. The most-cited works of Travis Hirschi were *A General Theory of Crime* (Gottfredson & Hirschi, 1990), with 98 citations, and *Causes of Delinquency* (Hirschi, 1969), with 57 citations.

Of these 6 scholars, Hirschi was the most specialized, because he had only 28 different works cited (an average of 9.7 citations per work) and 2 highly cited works which accounted for 57 % of all his citations. In contrast, Piquero was a versatile scholar, because he had 94 different works cited (an average of 2.9 cites per work) and his 2 most-cited works accounted for only 11 % of all his citations. Sampson was both specialized and versatile, because he had 101 different works cited (an average of 7.1 citations per work) and 2 highly cited works, but they only accounted for 17 % of his many citations.

Table 4.3 also shows the comparable rankings of these scholars in the 4 earlier time periods. Twenty-three scholars (77 %) were in the top 30 in 2001–2005, 19 (63 %) in 1996–1900, 16 (53 %) in 1991–1995, and 10 (33 %) in 1986–1990. All of the top ten scholars in 2001–2005, 7 of the top 10 scholars in 1996–2000, 8 of the top 10 scholars in 1991–1995, and 7 of the top 10 scholars in 1986–2000 survived to be in the top 10 in 2006–2010. Alfred Blumstein, David P. Farrington, Michael R. Gottfredson, and Travis Hirschi were among the 12 most-cited scholars in all 5 time periods. Robert J. Sampson advanced from 21 in 1986–1990 to 5 in 1991–1995 and 1 in 1996–2000, 2001–2005, and 2006–2010.

Alex R. Piquero advanced considerably (from 16 to 5) between 2001–2005 and 2006–2010, as did Robert Brame (from 28 to 13.5). The highest new entrants in 2006–2010 were D. Wayne Osgood (13.5), Mark Warr (25), and Shawn D. Bushway (26). Moving downwards from 2001–2005 to 2006–2010 were Robert Agnew (from 10 to 24) and Delbert S. Elliott (from 11 to 28). The highest-ranked scholars in 2001–2005 who were missing from the top 30 in 2006–2010 were David Huizinga (ranked 20 in 2001–2005) and Marvin D. Krohn (21).

4.4 *Justice Quarterly* (JQ)

In JQ in 2006–2010, 141 articles were published by a total of 347 individual authors, most of whom (326 or 94 %) were American. These articles contained a total of 18,325 cited authors, of which 813 were self-citations and 650 were coauthor citations. The 17,512 eligible cited authors (an average of 124 per article) could be compared with 15,097 in 2001–2005 (105 per article), 12,636 in 1996–2000 (84 per article) 9,188 in 1991–1995 (67 per article), and 9,393 in 1986–1990 (68 per article). Therefore, the number of cited authors per article increased by 82 % over this time period. However, it should be noted that, in 2010, JQ increased from 4 to 6 issues per year.

Table 4.4 shows the most-cited scholars in JQ in 2006–2010. The most-cited scholar, Robert J. Sampson, was cited 157 times. His most-cited work was "Neighborhoods and violent crime" (Sampson et al., 1997) which was cited 17 times. In total, 51 different works by Sampson were cited in 54 different articles (38 % of all JQ articles). The next 2 most-cited scholars, Francis T. Cullen and Alex R. Piquero, had 92 and 91 citations, respectively. The most highly-cited female scholars were Cassia C. Spohn (18.5) and Janet L. Lauritsen (25).

Table 4.4 also shows the comparable rankings of these scholars in JQ in the 4 earlier time periods. Sampson was also the most-cited scholar in 2001–2005, and his most-cited work then was *Crime in the Making* (Sampson & Laub, 1993). John L. Hagan was the most-cited scholar in 1996–2000, and his most-cited work then was "Changing conceptions of race" (Peterson & Hagan, 1984). Hagan's large number of citations was mainly a function of the large number of different works by him that were cited. Lawrence W. Sherman was the most-cited scholar in 1991–1995, and his most-cited work during that time period was "Hot spots of predatory crime" (Sherman, Gartin, & Buerger, 1989), but his high rank was again mainly attributable to his large number of different works cited. Francis T. Cullen was the most-cited scholar in 1986–1990, and his most-cited work then was *Reaffirming Rehabilitation* (Cullen & Gilbert, 1982), and again he was a versatile author. Cullen was among the most-cited 3 scholars in all 5 time periods, and Travis Hirschi was always among the most-cited 9 scholars. Thirty-five of the 51 most-cited scholars in JQ (69 %) had been ranked in the top 50 in 2001–2005, 26 (51 %) in 1996–2000, 18 (35 %) in 1991–1995, and 12 (24 %) in 1986–1990. Nine scholars were ranked in the top 50 in all 5 time periods and an additional 6 were ranked in the top 50 in 4 of the 5 time periods.

Robert J. Sampson advanced from 12.5 in 1991–1995 to 2 in 1996–2000 and 1 in 2001–2005 and 2006–2010. He was not among the 50 most-cited scholars in 1986–1990. Between 2001–2005 and 2006–2010, big advances were made by Ronald L. Akers (from 36 to 13) and Robert Agnew (from 30 to 16.5). The highest new entrants were Richard Tewksbury (9), Tom R. Tyler (22), and Ronald Weitzer (22). Moving downwards between 2001–2005 and 2006–2010 were Harold G. Grasmick (from 7 to 16.5), Robert J. Bursik (from 8 to 20), and Terence P. Thornberry (from 15 to 28.5). All of the top 12 scholars from 2001 to 2005 remained in the top 20 in 2006–2010; the highest-ranked scholars who did not survive were Daniel S. Nagin (ranked 13 in 2001–2005) and Theodore G. Chiricos (21).

Table 4.4 Most-cited scholars in *Justice Quarterly*

Rank in 2006–2010	Rank in 2001–2005	Rank in 1996–2000	Rank in 1991–1995	Rank in 1986–1990	Name	Cites
1	1	2	12.5	–	Robert J. Sampson	157
2	3	3	3	1	Francis T. Cullen[a]	92
3	9	–	–	–	Alex R. Piquero	91
4	12	–	–	–	Stephen W. Raudenbush	67
6.5	5	14.5	6	7.5	Michael R. Gottfredson	63
6.5	2	8.5	4.5	3	Travis Hirschi	63
6.5	4	23	–	–	John H. Laub	63
6.5	6	4	45	28	Raymond Paternoster	63
9	–	–	–	–	Richard Tewksbury[b]	59
10.5	10.5	29.5	19.5	28	David P. Farrington	56
10.5	18	34.5	45	–	Darrell J. Steffensmeier	56
12	10.5	17	1	18	Lawrence W. Sherman	55
13	36	–	19	15	Ronald L. Akers	50
14	18	1	2	9.5	John L. Hagan	48
15	28	–	27.5	–	Jeffrey A. Fagan	47
16.5	30	5	–	–	Robert Agnew	46
16.5	7	20.5	–	–	Harold G. Grasmick	46
18.5	23.5	46.5	38	–	Marvin D. Krohn	45
18.5	–	25.5	–	–	Cassia C. Spohn	45
20	8	8.5	–	–	Robert J. Bursik	44
22	41.5	–	–	–	Paul J. Mazerolle	42
22	–	–	–	–	Tom R. Tyler	42
22	–	–	–	–	Ronald Weitzer	42
25	39	24	–	–	Scott H. Decker	41
25	18	–	–	–	Janet L. Lauritsen	41
25	–	–	–	–	Travis C. Pratt	41
28.5	–	–	–	–	John H. Kramer	40
28.5	30	–	–	–	Steven F. Messner	40
28.5	34	40	–	–	Terrie E. Moffitt	40
28.5	15	40	–	–	Terence P. Thornberry	40
31	–	13	–	–	Ralph B. Taylor	39
32.5	44	–	–	–	Robert Brame	38
32.5	47.5	–	–	–	David L. Weisburd	38
34	34	–	38	–	Rolf Loeber	37
35	21	46.5	–	–	Charles R. Tittle	35
36	–	–	–	–	Stephen D. Mastrofski	34
38	–	–	–	–	Celesta A. Albonetti	33
38	–	–	–	–	Finn-Aage Esbensen[c]	33
38	26.5	25.5	–	–	William J. Wilson	33
42	47.5	46.5	19.5	4	Alfred Blumstein	32
42	16	11.5	8.5	–	David Huizinga	32

(continued)

Table 4.4 (continued)

Rank in 2006–2010	Rank in 2001–2005	Rank in 1996–2000	Rank in 1991–1995	Rank in 1986–1990	Name	Cites
42	50.5	–	–	28	Alan J. Lizotte	32
42	21	8.5	15	5	Wesley G. Skogan	32
42	–	8.5	23.5	–	Douglas A. Smith	32
45	–	–	–	–	Richard B. Felson	31
46	–	27	38	48.5	Christy A. Visher	30
47.5	47.5	–	–	–	Kenneth C. Land	29
47.5	14	–	–	–	Mark Warr	29
50	–	–	–	–	Elijah Anderson	28
50	–	–	–	–	Eric P. Baumer	28
50	–	–	–	–	Richard Rosenfeld	28

[a]Editor, 1987–1989
[b]Editor, 2008–2010
[c]Editor 1999–2001

4.5 Journal of Criminal Justice (JCJ)

In JCJ in 2006–2010, 373 articles were published by a total of 893 authors, 91 % of whom (816) were American. The non-American authors were most commonly from Canada (19) and Australia (9). These articles contained a total of 41,508 cited authors, of which 1,485 were self-citations and 1,276 were coauthor citations. The 40,023 eligible cited authors (an average of 107 per article) may be compared with 19,274 (80 per article) in 2001–2005, 12,744 in 1996–2000 (65 per article), 9,716 in 1991–1995 (50 per article), and 7,234 in 1986–1990 (40 per article), showing that the number of cited authors per article increased by 168 % over this time period.

Table 4.5 shows the most-cited scholars in JCJ in 2006–2010. The most-cited scholar, Francis T. Cullen, was cited 354 times. He had 123 different works cited in 155 different articles (42 % of all JCJ articles), making him an extremely versatile author. His most-cited work was "The empirical status of Gottfredson and Hirschi's general theory of crime" (Pratt & Cullen, 2000), which was cited 27 times. The next most highly-cited scholars were Alex R. Piquero and Robert J. Sampson, who were cited 246 and 223 times, respectively. The most-cited female scholars were Terrie E. Moffitt (ranked 15.5) and Bonnie S. Fisher (29).

Table 4.5 also shows the comparable rankings of these scholars in JCJ in the previous 4 time periods. Cullen was also the most-cited scholar in 2001–2005 and 1996–2000, and his most-cited work in these years was "The social dimensions of correctional officer stress" (Cullen, Link, Wolfe, & Frank, 1985). Again, his large number of citations was mainly attributable to the large number of his different works that were cited. John L. Hagan was the most-cited scholar in 1991–1995. His most-cited work then was "Extra-legal attributes and criminal sentencing" (Hagan, 1974), and again his large number of citations was mainly a function of his large

Table 4.5 Most-cited scholars in *Journal of Criminal Justice*

Rank in 2006–2010	Rank in 2001–2005	Rank in 1996–2000	Rank in 1991–1995	Rank in 1986–1990	Name	Cites
1	1	1	2	17.5	Francis T. Cullen	354
2	15	–	–	–	Alex R. Piquero	246
3	2	27.5	23	–	Robert J. Sampson	223
4	28	13.5	–	–	Robert Agnew	156
5	3	4	34	–	David P. Farrington	154
6	5	2	3.5	–	Travis Hirschi	137
7	20	–	–	–	Paul J. Mazerolle	116
8	4	–	–	–	Raymond Paternoster	114
9	9.5	3	9	31	Michael R. Gottfredson	105
10	29.5	5.5	7.5	3	Lawrence W. Sherman	104
11	14	–	–	–	John H. Laub	102
12	9.5	–	–	–	Harold G. Grasmick	95
13	8	–	–	–	Daniel S. Nagin	94
14	–	–	–	–	Travis C. Pratt	92
15.5	32	–	–	–	Steven F. Messner	90
15.5	6	–	–	–	Terrie E. Moffitt	90
17	–	–	–	–	Tom R. Tyler	89
18.5	24.5	13.5	1	7	John L. Hagan	87
18.5	–	–	–	–	Darrell J. Steffensmeier	87
20	7	–	–	–	Robert J. Bursik	83
21	–	–	–	–	Ronald Weitzer	80
22	45	38.5	–	–	Scott H. Decker	76
23.5	–	9	–	–	Ronald L. Akers	75
23.5	45	–	–	–	Michael D. Reisig	75
25.5	12	13.5	23	17.5	Wesley G. Skogan	74
25.5	50.5	46.5	48	–	Charles R. Tittle	74
27	18	–	–	–	Rolf Loeber	73
28	20	7.5	14.5	4.5	Alfred Blumstein	72
29	–	–	–	–	Bonnie S. Fisher	71
30.5	–	–	–	–	Terance D. Miethe	69
30.5	–	46.5	–	–	Cassia C. Spohn	69
32	11	–	–	–	Robert E. Worden	68
33.5	–	–	–	–	Marvin D. Krohn	67
33.5	32	–	–	–	Stephen W. Raudenbush	67
35	26.5	–	–	–	Steven D. Mastrofski	66
36	39	–	–	–	Mark Warr	64
37	–	–	–	–	Robin S. Engel	63
38	–	–	–	–	John P. Wright	62

(continued)

Table 4.5 (continued)

Rank in 2006–2010	Rank in 2001–2005	Rank in 1996–2000	Rank in 1991–1995	Rank in 1986–1990	Name	Cites
39.5	16.5	35	–	–	Doris L. MacKenzie	61
39.5	–	–	23	–	Terence P. Thornberry	61
41	–	–	–	–	Steven A. Tuch	59
42	22.5	11	6	22.5	Joan Petersilia	58
43	–	–	–	–	Richard Rosenfeld	56
44	20	–	–	–	Robert Brame	55
45.5	16.5	38.5	–	–	James Frank	54
45.5	22.5	18.5	28	–	Samuel Walker	54
47	–	–	–	–	Avshalom Caspi	53
48.5	13	–	28	–	Geoffrey P. Alpert	52
48.5	–	35	48	–	Paul Gendreau	52

number of different works cited. Robert M. Regoli was the most-cited scholar in 1986–1990. His most-cited work then was "Police cynicism and professionalism" (Lotz & Regoli, 1977), and again he was a versatile author.

The most-cited scholars in JCJ tended to be more variable than in the previous 4 journals. No scholar was in the top 10 in all 5 time periods, although 5 were in the top 30 in all 5 time periods (Alfred Blumstein, Francis T. Cullen, John L. Hagan, Lawrence W. Sherman, and Wesley G. Skogan). Thirty-three of the 49 most-cited scholars in 2006–2010 (67 %) had been ranked in the top 50 in 2001–2005, 19 (39 %) in 1996–2000, 15 (31 %) in 1991–1995, and only 7 (14 %) in 1986–1990. Seven scholars were in the top 50 in all 5 time periods and 5 additional scholars were ranked in the top 50 in 4 of the 5 time periods.

Between 2001–2005 and 2006–2010, big advances were made by Alex R. Piquero (from 15 to 2), Robert Agnew (from 28 to 4), and Paul J. Mazerolle (from 20 to 7). The highest new entrants were Travis C. Pratt (14), Tom R. Tyler (17), and Darrell J. Steffensmeier (18.5). Moving downwards from 2001–2005 to 2006–2010 were Robert J. Bursik (from 7 to 20), Wesley G. Skogan (from 12 to 25.5), and Robert E. Worden (from 11 to 32). All of the top 23 scholars in 2001–2005 survived to be in the top 49 in 2006–2010; the highest-ranked scholars who did not survive were David H. Bayley (ranked 24.5 in 2001–2005) and James Q. Wilson (26.5).

4.6 *Criminal Justice and Behavior* (CJB)

In CJB in 2006–2010, 366 articles were published by a total of 1,154 authors, only 68 % of whom (782) were American. CJB was clearly the most international of the 6 American journals. There were a large number of Canadian authors (167), as well as 80 from the United Kingdom, 26 from Australia, 21 from Sweden, 19 from the Netherlands, and 18 from Germany. These articles contained a total of 48,005 cited authors, of which 2,961 were self-citations and 3,175 were coauthor citations. The 45,044 eligible cited authors (an average of 123 per article) could be compared with 14,913 in 2001–2005 (96 per article), 10,400 in 1996–2000 (76 per article), 7,442 in 1991–1995 (55 per article), and 6,267 in 1986–1990 (46 per article), so that the number of cited authors per article in CJB almost tripled over this time period. In 2000, CJB increased its frequency of publication from 4 to 6 issues per year, and in 2007 it began publishing monthly.

Table 4.6 shows the most-cited scholars in CJB in 2006–2010. The most-cited scholar, Robert D. Hare, was cited 277 times, and his most-cited work was *The Psychopathy Checklist—Revised* (Hare, 2003) in its various editions, which was cited 78 times. Hare had 65 different works cited in 77 articles (21 % of all CJB articles), so he was both specialized and versatile. Eight of the top 10 scholars (all except Terrie E. Moffitt and Francis T. Cullen) were Canadian researchers known for their work on the effectiveness of correctional treatment, psychopathy, and/or risk assessment. Terrie E. Moffitt (5) and Marnie E. Rice (6) were the most-cited female authors.

Table 4.6 also shows the comparable rankings of these scholars in CJB in the 4 previous time periods. Don A. Andrews was the most-cited scholar in 2001–2005 and 1996–2000, and his most-cited work was *The Psychology of Criminal Conduct* (Andrews & Bonta, 1994), in its various editions. William L. Marshall was the most-cited scholar in 1991–1995. His most-cited works then were "The long-term evaluation of a behavioral treatment program for child molesters" (Marshall & Barbaree, 1988) and "Erectile responses among heterosexual child molesters, father-daughter incest offenders and matched nonoffenders" (Barbaree & Marshall, 1989). Marshall's large number of citations was mainly a function of his large number of different works cited, which may be related to the fact that in 1991–1995 CJB published a number of articles focusing on sex offenders. Edwin I. Megargee was the most-cited scholar in 1986–1990. He was a specialized author whose most-cited work then was *Classifying Criminal Offenders* (Megargee & Bohn, 1979). Only Robert D. Hare and John T. Monahan were among the most-cited 20 scholars in all 5 time periods. Twenty-four scholars (49 %) had been ranked in the top 50 in 2001–2005, 23 (47 %) in 1996–2000, 13 (27 %) in 1991–1995, and only 9 (18 %) in 1986–1990, showing the changing focus of CJB over time. Only 6 scholars were ranked in the top 50 in all 5 time periods; 7 additional scholars were ranked in the top 50 in 4 of the 5 time periods.

Between 2001–2005 and 2006–2010, big advances were made by R. Karl Hanson (from 14.5 to 4), Terrie E. Moffitt (from 37.5 to 5), and David P. Farrington (from 26.5 to 11). The highest new entrants were Paul J. Frick (13), Alex R. Piquero (14.5), and D. Dwayne Simpson (16). Moving downwards between 2001–2005 and 2006–2010 were John T. Monahan (from 7 to 20.5) and Catherine A. Cormier (from 17 to 32.5). All of the top 10 scholars in 2001–2005 survived to be in the top 49 in 2006–2010; the highest-ranked scholars who did not survive were Christopher D. Webster (ranked 11 in 2001–2005) and Loren H. Roth (16).

Table 4.6 Most-cited scholars in *Criminal Justice and Behavior*

Rank in 2006–2010	Rank in 2001–2005	Rank in 1996–2000	Rank in 1991–1995	Rank in 1986–1990	Name	Cites
1	3	3	15	6	Robert D. Hare	277
2	1	1	2	–	Don A. Andrews	227
3	2	2	8	–	James L. Bonta	226
4	13.5	–	–	–	R. Karl Hanson	222
5	37.5	9.5	–	–	Terrie E. Moffitt	202
6	4	4	19	–	Marnie E. Rice	158
7	13.5	11.5	27.5	16.5	Francis T. Cullen	153
8	5	5	15	–	Grant T. Harris	150
9	9	7	38	3	Paul Gendreau	141
10	6	6	3	28.5	Vernon L. Quinsey	137
11	26.5	18	47	–	David P. Farrington	129
12	18	30.5	–	–	Rolf Loeber	124
13	–	–	–	–	Paul J. Frick	121
14.5	8	8	–	–	Stephen D. Hart	114
14.5	–	–	–	–	Alex R. Piquero	114
16	–	–	–	–	D. Dwayne Simpson	113
17	–	–	–	–	Avshalom Caspi	105
18	28	30.5	–	–	Claire E. Goggin	93
19	–	–	–	–	David Thornton	90
20.5	15	30.5	–	–	Thomas Grisso	89
20.5	7	16.5	10.5	7.5	John T. Monahan	89
22	–	9.5	47	16.5	Travis Hirschi	84
23.5	–	–	–	–	John F. Edens	82
23.5	–	–	–	–	Glenn D. Walters	82
25	46	50.5	1	40.5	William L. Marshall	81
26	–	–	–	–	Kenneth A. Dodge	79
27.5	–	–	–	–	Richard Rogers	78
27.5	–	–	–	–	Robert J. Sampson	78
29	19	13	–	–	Robert D. Hoge	76
30	34	–	–	–	Paul E. Meehl	73
31	–	–	–	–	Adrian Raine	72
32.5	17	30.5	–	–	Catherine A. Cormier	71
32.5	–	–	–	–	Magda Stouthamer-Loeber	71
35.5	24.5	25.5	–	–	Adelle E. Forth	69
35.5	–	21.5	–	–	Michael R. Gottfredson	69
35.5	–	–	–	–	Edward J. Latessa	69
35.5	12	–	–	–	Edward P. Mulvey	69
38	–	–	–	–	Tony Ward	68
39	–	–	–	–	Donald R. Lynam	65
40	–	–	–	–	Travis C. Pratt	64

(continued)

Table 4.6 (continued)

Rank in 2006–2010	Rank in 2001–2005	Rank in 1996–2000	Rank in 1991–1995	Rank in 1986–1990	Name	Cites
41	–	–	–	–	R. James Blair	63
42	–	–	–	–	Kevin Knight	61
43.5	–	–	–	–	Daniel S. Nagin	60
43.5	–	–	–	–	Laurence Steinberg	60
45	22	–	–	–	Kevin S. Douglas	59
47	–	–	–	–	Scott O. Lilienfeld	57
47	–	–	–	–	Kelly E. Morton-Gourgon	57
47	–	25.5	23	7.5	Hans Toch	57
49	10	23.5	–	10	Henry J. Steadman	56

4.7 Most-Cited Scholars in Three Criminal Justice Journals

A combined measure of influence based on all 3 criminal justice journals was then calculated, using the methodology described earlier. Table 4.7 shows the 30 most-cited scholars on this combined measure. Francis T. Cullen, Alex R. Piquero, David P. Farrington, Robert J. Sampson, and Travis Hirschi were the most-cited scholars. Terrie E. Moffitt (6) and Cassia C. Spohn (25) were the only female scholars on this list. Only 9 scholars were among the top 50 scholars in all 3 journals, so it is clear that there is less agreement on the most-cited scholars among the 3 criminal justice journals than among the 3 criminology journals. Cullen was in the top 7 in all 3 journals, and Farrington was in the top 11 in all 3 journals.

We also determined the most-cited works of the most-cited scholars in these 3 journals. For Francis T. Cullen, these were "The empirical status of Gottfredson and Hirschi's general theory of crime" (Pratt & Cullen, 2000), with 28 citations, and "Does correctional treatment work?" (Andrews et al., 1990), with 19 citations. For Alex R. Piquero, these were "Using the correct statistical test for the equality of regression coefficients" (Paternoster et al., 1998), with 19 citations, and "The criminal career paradigm" (Piquero et al., 2003), with 15 citations. For David P. Farrington, these were "The criminal career paradigm" (Piquero et al., 2003), with 22 citations, and "Age and crime" (Farrington, 1986), with 12 citations.

The most-cited works of Robert J. Sampson were *Crime in the Making* (Sampson & Laub, 1993), with 41 citations, and "Neighborhoods and violent crime" (Sampson et al., 1997), with 40 citations. The most-cited works of Travis Hirschi were *A General Theory of Crime* (Gottfredson & Hirschi, 1990), with 77 citations, and *Causes of Delinquency* (Hirschi, 1969), with 32 citations. The most-cited works of Terrie E. Moffitt were "Adolescence-limited and life-course-persistent antisocial behavior" (Moffitt, 1993), with 68 citations, and "The interaction between

Table 4.7 Most-cited scholars in three American criminal justice journals

Rank in 2006–2010	Rank in 2001–2005	Rank in 1996–2000	Rank in 1991–1995	Rank in 1986–1990	Name	Score in JQ	Score in JCJ	Score in CJB	Total
1	1	1	1	4	Francis T. Cullen	49	50	44	143
2	12	–	–	–	Alex R. Piquero	48	49	36.5	133.5
3	2	4	17	–	David P. Farrington	40.5	46	40	126.5
4	3	12	11	–	Robert J. Sampson	50	48	23.5	121.5
5	4	2	3	16	Travis Hirschi	44.5	45	29	118.5
6	13	17	–	–	Terrie E. Moffitt	22.5	35.5	46	104
7	6	3	6	12	Michael R. Gottfredson	44.5	42	15.5	102
8	5	24.5	–	–	Raymond Paternoster	44.5	43	0	87.5
9	9	–	–	–	John H. Laub	44.5	40	0	84.5
10	28.5	7	–	–	Robert Agnew	34.5	47	0	81.5
11.5	10	–	–	–	Rolf Loeber	17	24	39	80
11.5	15	8.5	4	13	Lawrence W. Sherman	39	41	0	80
13	–	–	–	–	Travis C. Pratt	26	37	11	74
14	8	–	–	–	Harold G. Grasmick	34.5	39	0	73.5
15.5	–	–	–	–	Paul J. Mazerolle	29	44	0	73
15.5	–	–	–	–	Darrell J. Steffensmeier	40.5	32.5	0	73
17	16	5	2	10	John L. Hagan	37	32.5	0	69.5
18	–	–	–	27	Ronald L. Akers	38	27.5	0	65.5
19	17	–	–	–	Stephen W. Raudenbush	47	17.5	0	64.5
20	–	–	–	–	Tom R. Tyler	29	34	0	63
21	7	–	–	–	Robert J. Bursik	31	31	0	62
22	–	–	–	–	Ronald Weitzer	29	30	0	59
23	–	–	–	–	Steven F. Messner	22.5	35.5	0	58

4.7 Most-Cited Scholars in Three Criminal Justice Journals

24	Scott H. Decker	–	–	–	26	29	0	55
25	Cassia C. Spohn	–	–	–	32.5	20.5	0	53
26.5	Robert D. Hare	23	22.5	–	0	0	50	50
26.5	Marvin D. Krohn	–	–	–	32.5	17.5	0	50
28	Don A. Andrews	20	19	18	0	0	49	49
29	James L. Bonta	21.5	20.5	–	0	0	48	48
30	R. Karl Hanson	–	–	–	0	0	47	47

impulsivity and neighborhood context on offending" (Lynam, Caspi, Moffitt, Wikstrom, Loeber, & Novak, 2000), with 12 citations.

Four of these 6 scholars (Piquero, Farrington, Sampson, and Hirschi) were also among the 6 most-cited scholars in the 3 criminology journals. It was interesting that their most-cited works were the same in both sets of journals. In total, 16 of the 30 most-cited scholars in the 3 criminal justice journals were also among the 30 most-cited scholars in the 3 criminology journals. There is clearly considerable overlap between citation patterns in criminology and criminal justice.

Of the 6 most-cited scholars in the 3 criminal justice journals, Hirschi was the most specialized, because he had only 26 different works cited (an average of 10.9 citations per work) and 2 highly cited works (accounting for 38 % of all his citations). In contrast, Piquero was versatile, because he had 116 different works cited (an average of 3.9 citations per work) and his 2 most-cited works accounted for only 8 % of his citations. As before, Sampson was both specialized and versatile, because he had 78 different works cited (an average of 5.9 citations per work) and 2 highly cited works, but they only accounted for 18 % of his many citations. Cullen and Farrington were also versatile authors, while Moffitt was versatile but had 1 highly cited work (accounting for 20 % of her citations).

Table 4.7 also shows the comparable rankings of these scholars in the 4 earlier time periods. Nineteen scholars (63 %) were in the top 30 in 2001–2005, 13 (43 %) in 1996–2000, 8 (27 %) in 1991–1995, and 6 (20 %) in 1986–1990. Francis T. Cullen was top in 4 of the time periods and ranked 4 in 1986–1990. Only 5 scholars (Cullen, Hirschi, Gottfredson, Lawrence W. Sherman, and John L. Hagan) were among the most-cited scholars in all 5 time periods, and an additional 3 (Farrington, Sampson, and Don A. Andrews) were among the most-cited in 4 of the 5 time periods.

Alex R. Piquero advanced considerably (from 12 to 2) from 2001–2005 to 2006–2010, as did Robert Agnew (from 28.5 to 10). The highest new entrants in 2006–2010 were Travis C. Pratt (13), Paul J. Mazerolle (15.5), and Darrell J. Steffensmeier (15.5). Robert J. Bursik moved downwards (from 7 to 21). The highest-ranked scholars in 2001–2005 who were missing from the top 30 in 2006–2010 were Daniel S. Nagin (ranked 11 in 2001–2005) and Wesley G. Skogan (14).

4.8 Most-Cited Scholars in Six American Journals

A combined measure of influence in all 6 journals in 2006–2010 was calculated by adding scores in the 3 criminology journals and scores in the 3 criminal justice journals. Table 4.8 shows the most-cited 50 scholars on this combined measure. Only 7 scholars (Francis T. Cullen, David P. Farrington, Michael R. Gottfredson, Travis Hirschi, Terrie E. Moffitt, Alex R. Piquero, and Robert J. Sampson) were ranked among the 50 most-cited scholars in all 6 journals. Table 4.8 shows that the 5 most-cited scholars on the combined measure were Sampson, Piquero, Cullen, Farrington, and Hirschi. Moffitt (6) was the highest-ranked female scholar.

4.8 Most-Cited Scholars in Six American Journals

Table 4.8 Most-cited scholars in six major American journals

Rank in 2006–2010	Rank in 2001–2005	Rank in 1996–2000	Rank in 1991–1995	Rank in 1986–1990	Name	CRM	CJ	Total
1	2	4	3	42	Robert J. Sampson	150	121.5	271.5
2	12	–	–	–	Alex R. Piquero	134.5	133.5	268
3	4	13	14	13	Francis T. Cullen	123.5	143	266.5
4	1	3	6	14	David P. Farrington	135	126.5	261.5
5	3	1	1	4	Travis Hirschi	133.5	118.5	252
6	8	23	–	–	Terrie E. Moffitt	128.5	104	232.5
7	9	11	36	–	John H. Laub	140	84.5	224.5
8	6	2	2	5	Michael R. Gottfredson	121	102	223
9	5	19	23	39	Raymond Paternoster	129	87.5	216.5
10	13	–	–	–	Stephen W. Raudenbush	128	64.5	192.5
11	7	21	27	–	Daniel S. Nagin	137	45.5	182.5
12	18	34	–	–	Darrell J. Steffensmeier	85	73	158
13	11	28	30	–	Rolf Loeber	69.5	80	149.5
14	16	10	4	3	Alfred Blumstein	116.5	32	148.5
15	10	15	29	–	Robert J. Bursik	86	62	148
16	14	8	–	–	Robert Agnew	65.5	81.5	147
17	15	24	31	–	Harold G. Grasmick	72	73.5	145.5
18	27	33	–	–	Steven F. Messner	74	58	132
19	29	–	–	–	Robert Brame	105	25.5	130.5
20	24	18	15	25	Lawrence W. Sherman	46	80	126
21	19	6	8	6	John L. Hagan	46	69.5	115.5
22	28	–	–	–	Avshalom Caspi	73.5	38	111.5
23	20	29	–	–	Kenneth C. Land	104	3.5	107.5
24	37	–	–	–	D. Wayne Osgood	105	0	105
25	–	–	–	–	Travis C. Pratt	30.5	74	104.5

(continued)

Table 4.8 (continued)

Rank in 2006–2010	Rank in 2001–2005	Rank in 1996–2000	Rank in 1991–1995	Rank in 1986–1990	Name	CRM	CJ	Total
26	–	12	18	18	Ronald L. Akers	34.5	65.5	100
27	23	–	–	–	Paul J. Mazerolle	25.5	73	98.5
28	–	38	20	45.5	Marcus Felson	84.5	0	84.5
29	33	–	–	–	Mark Warr	63.5	18.5	82
30	25.5	25.5	22	29	Marvin D. Krohn	30	50	80
31	25.5	20	34	–	Terence P. Thornberry	42.5	34	76.5
32	–	–	–	–	Cassia C. Spohn	22	53	75
33	32	22	5	10	Lawrence E. Cohen	71.5	0	71.5
34	31	32	28	30	Charles R. Tittle	24.5	41.5	66
35	–	–	–	–	David L. Weisburd	45.5	18.5	64
36	–	–	–	–	Tom R. Tyler	0	63	63
37	–	–	–	–	Shawn D. Bushway	62.5	0	62.5
38	–	–	–	–	Ronald Weitzer	0	59	59
39	36	–	–	–	Janet L. Lauritsen	30.5	26	56.5
40	–	–	–	–	Richard Rosenfeld	47	9	56
41.5	–	–	–	–	Scott H. Decker	0	55	55
41.5	–	–	–	–	Jeffrey D. Morenoff	55	0	55
43	17	5	9	9	Delbert S. Elliott	54.5	0	54.5
44	–	30	11	7	Jacqueline Cohen	53.5	0	53.5
45	–	41	–	–	Terance D. Miethe	31	20.5	51.5
46	40.5	–	–	–	Ralph B. Taylor	31	20	51
47	44	45	–	–	Robert D. Hare	0	50	50
48	21	7	7	–	David Huizinga	40.5	9	49.5
49	39	42	38	–	Don A. Andrews	0	49	49
50	43.5	–	–	–	James L. Bonta	0	48	48

CRM = 3 criminology journals
CJ = 3 criminal justice journals

Table 4.8 also shows the comparable rankings of these scholars in the 4 previous time periods. Travis Hirschi and Michael R. Gottfredson were among the most-cited 8 scholars in all 5 time periods, while Francis T. Cullen, David P. Farrington, and Alfred Blumstein were among the most-cited 16 scholars in all 5 time periods. Thirty-seven scholars (74 %) were in the top 50 in 2001–2005, 31 (62 %) in 1996–2000, 24 (48 %) in 1991–1995, and 16 (32 %) in 1986–1990. Thirteen scholars were among the most-cited scholars in all 5 time periods and an additional 11 were among the most-cited scholars in 4 of the 5 time periods.

Between 2001–2005 and 2006–2010, Alex R. Piquero advanced considerably (from 12 to 2), as did Steven F. Messner (from 29 to 19) and D. Wayne Osgood (from 37 to 24). The highest new entrants in 2006–2010 were Travis C. Pratt (25) and Cassia C. Spohn (32). All of the top 21 scholars in 2001–2005 survived to be in the top 50 in 2006–2010; the highest-ranked scholars who did not survive were Wesley G. Skogan (ranked 22 in 2001–2005) and William J. Wilson (30).

Our results can be used to study citation careers (see also Cohn & Farrington, 2012b). For example, the most-cited scholar in 1986–1990, Marvin E. Wolfgang, declined to 10 in 1991–1995 and 31 in 1996–2000 before dropping out of the table. He died in 1998. The second most-cited scholar in 1986–1990, Michael J. Hindelang, declined to 13 in 1991–1995 and 27 in 1996–2000 before dropping out of the table. He died in 1982. In contrast, Robert J. Sampson was ranked only 42 in 1986–1990 but he advanced to 3 in 1991–1995, 4 in 1996–2000, 2 in 2001–2005, and 1 in 2006–2010. An even younger scholar, Alex R. Piquero, first entered the table at 12 in 2001–2005 and then advanced to 2 in 2006–2010.

4.9 Conclusion

The main limitation of our research is that it is based on citations in only a small number of central American criminology and criminal justice journals that were being published in 1986. As a result, it may underestimate the influence of those scholars who publish mainly in other journals. For comparability with previous studies, we have reported the total number of citations, but the prevalence of citations (the number of different articles in which a scholar is cited) may be a better measure of scholarly influence.

This study of citation trends in 6 major journals over 25 years shows how the influence of an older generation of scholars gradually was being replaced by the influence of the next generation. The "Kings" of the 1980s, such as Alfred Blumstein and Jacqueline Cohen, were gradually being cited less. Deceased scholars such as Michael J. Hindelang and Marvin Wolfgang were also being cited less.

Robert J. Sampson, who was once taught by Alfred Blumstein, was the most highly-cited scholar in 3 American criminology journals in 2006–2010. Two other scholars who were greatly influenced by Blumstein (Daniel S. Nagin and David P. Farrington) were also among the most highly-cited scholars in these journals. Thus, as Blumstein's own citations decreased, his influence lived on in the next generation of scholars. The most-cited scholars in these journals still tended to focus on longitudinal/criminal career research and/or criminological theories. There was generally good agreement among the 3 criminology journals on the most-cited scholars.

The most-cited scholars in 2 of the 3 American criminal justice journals (JQ and JCJ) overlapped with those in American criminology journals, with the addition of some scholars who specialized in criminal justice topics such as rehabilitation and law enforcement (e.g., Francis T. Cullen and Lawrence W. Sherman). However, the most highly-cited scholars in CJB tended to be Canadian researchers who focused on the effectiveness of rehabilitative treatment, psychopathy, or risk assessment.

The most-cited works of the most-cited authors show that some authors (e.g., Robert J. Sampson, Travis Hirschi) were specialized, because they had a large number of citations of 1 or 2 seminal works, usually books and often theoretical in nature. Other authors were versatile, because they had many different works cited a few times each. Therefore, there are 2 different ways in which scholarly influence operates in criminology and criminal justice.

This analysis of citations over 25 years shows the emerging influence of a new generation of younger scholars, notably Robert J. Sampson, Raymond Paternoster, Daniel S. Nagin, Terrie E. Moffitt, John H. Laub, and, most recently, Alex R. Piquero. If these analyses could be continued for many more years, the complete trajectories of criminological citation careers could be documented, and the extent to which citation careers could be predicted at different stages could be investigated. These kinds of analyses would greatly advance knowledge about the waxing and waning of scholarly influence in criminology.

Chapter 5
Most-Cited Scholars in 20 Journals

As discussed in Chapter 1, one concern that has been raised about Cohn and Farrington's method of citation analysis is that it uses only a small number of prestigious mainstream criminology and criminal justice (CCJ) journals. In response to this, they increased the number of journals from 9 to 20. The process of selecting these journals is described in Chapter 2. This chapter examines the most-cited scholars in 2010 in 20 journals: 5 American criminology journals, 5 American criminal justice journals, 5 international criminology journals, and 5 international criminal justice journals. Exactly the same methods were used in all analyses, so that valid comparisons over time could be made. Comparisons are made with the results from 4 earlier years (1990, 1995, 2000, 2005) so that changes in the influence and prestige of scholars during the past 20 years can be documented. The most-cited works of the most-cited scholars are also listed.

5.1 Citations in 20 Journals

Table 5.1 summarizes key statistics for the 20 journals, including the number of articles published in 2010, the number of authors of these articles, the percentage of these authors who were located in the United States, and the total number of eligible cited scholars in the journal (excluding self-citations and institutional authors). In the 5 American criminology journals, there were a total of 260 articles, with 726 authors (79 % of whom were American) and a total of 29,020 cited scholars (an average of 112 per article). The 5 American criminal justice journals contained a total of 237 articles written by 589 authors (92 % of whom were American) and a total of 25,283 cited scholars (an average of 107 per article). In the 5 international criminology journals, there were 178 articles, with 308 authors (14 % American) and a total of 12,185 cited authors (an average of 68 per article). Finally, in the 5 international criminal justice journals, there were 180 articles written by 486 authors (70 % American) and a total of 20,877 cited scholars (an average of 116 per article).

Table 5.1 Articles, authors, and citations

Title	Articles	Authors	% US	Citations
American criminology journals				
Criminology (CRIM)	36	90	84.4	4,635
Journal of Quantitative Criminology (JQC)	31	62	75.8	3,344
Journal of Research in Crime and Delinquency (JRCD)	20	53	84.9	2,613
Journal of Interpersonal Violence (JIV)	121	377	65.2	12,159
Violence and Victims (VAV)	52	144	83.3	6,269
Total	260	726	78.7	29,020
American criminal justice journals				
Justice Quarterly (JQ)	34	87	94.3	4,377
Journal of Criminal Justice (JCJ)	135	335	89.9	15,883
Crime and Delinquency (CAD)	24	61	86.9	2,445
Criminal Justice Review (CJR)	22	57	100	1,969
Federal Probation (FP)	22	49	89.8	609
Total	237	589	92.2	25,283
International criminology journals				
Australian and New Zealand Journal of Criminology (ANZ)	25	41	12.2	1,925
British Journal of Criminology (BJC)	55	104	15.4	4,499
Canadian Journal of Criminology and Criminal Justice (CJC)	25	57	5.3	1,413
Crime, Law, and Social Change (CLSC)	47	61	36.1	2,715
Criminologie (CRGE)	26	45	0	1,633
Total	178	308	13.8	12,185
International criminal justice journals				
Crime and Justice (CAJ)	9	15	73.3	2,662
Criminal Justice and Behavior (CJB)	71	235	64.7	9,513
International Journal of Comparative and Applied Criminal Justice (IJCA)	17	28	67.9	1,119
International Journal of Offender Therapy and Comparative Criminology (IJOT)	59	181	53.0	6,690
Social Justice (SJ)	24	27	88.9	893
Total	180	486	69.6	20,877
Total American journals	497	1,315	85.5	54,303
Total international journals	358	794	41.7	33,062
Total criminology journals	438	1,034	46.3	41,205
Total criminal justice journals	417	1,075	80.9	46,160
Total for all 20 journals	855	2,109	63.6	87,365

Note: % US shows the percent of authors located in the United States

In 2010, this research examined 855 articles in these 20 journals (an average of 43 articles per journal) with 2,109 authors (64 % American, 105 per journal) and 87,365 citations (an average of 4,368 cited scholars per journal, or 102 per article).

The number of articles, authors, and citations in these 20 journals has increased dramatically over the years. When this research was first conducted for the year 1990, there were 503 articles (an average of 25 per journal), 857 authors (66 %

American, 43 per journal), and 23,697 citations (1,185 per journal, or 47 per article). Over 20 years, the number of articles has increased by 70 %, the number of authors by 146 %, and the number of citations by 269 %. The average number of citations per article has more than doubled.

5.2 Most-Cited Scholars in Each Journal

Table 5.2 shows the 5 most-cited scholars in each of the 20 journals in 2010. In CRIM, for example, the most-cited scholar was Robert J. Sampson, with 90 citations, followed by Stephen W. Raudenbush (39), Daniel S. Nagin (36), John H. Laub (30), and Raymond Paternoster (26). Robert J. Sampson was the most-cited scholar in 5 of the 20 journals, Francis T. Cullen was most-cited in 3 journals, and Murray A. Straus was most-cited in 2 journals. Robert J. Sampson was among the 5 most-cited scholars in 8 of these journals, while Francis T. Cullen appeared 5 times, and David P. Farrington and Alex R. Piquero each appeared 4 times in Table 5.2. The most-cited scholars in each journal reflect the different interests of the authors of each journal, for example, the most-cited scholars in SJ were rarely cited in CRIM, and vice versa.

It is clear from Table 5.2 that even the most-cited scholars in a journal or group of journals account for only a small fraction of the total number of citations in that journal or group of journals. For example, Robert J. Sampson, the most highly-cited scholar in CRIM, accounted for approximately 1.9 % of all citations in that journal in 2010. However, citations are highly skewed (Hamilton, 1990, 1991; Laband & Piette, 1994), and most scholars and works are never cited or are cited only once or twice. There is a clear difference between being cited once and being cited 90 times, as Sampson was in 2010 in CRIM. In fact, Sampson was cited in 74 % of all the articles in CRIM in 2010 (26 out of 35 articles; he was a coauthor of 1 article and his self-citations in that work were not counted). Thus, the vast majority of scholars publishing in CRIM in 2010 were sufficiently impacted by Sampson's work to cite him in their research. Therefore, while the most-cited scholar in a journal may account for a relatively small fraction of citations overall, a large number of citations is nevertheless an objective indicator of influence.

5.3 Most-Cited Scholars in Five Journals

In order to compare the citations of scholars in each of the 20 journals, the most-cited scholars in each journal were ranked and given a score of 26 minus their ranking. Generally, this meant that those scholars who were ranked from 1 to 25 in each journal (according to their citations) received scores ranging from 25 to 1 (respectively). However, more (or fewer) than 25 scholars could score in a given journal if there were ties. For example, in JQC, Robert J. Sampson, the most-cited scholar,

Table 5.2 Most-cited scholars in each journal

American criminology journals

CRIM	R.J. Sampson (90); S.W. Raudenbush (39); D.S. Nagin (36); J.H. Laub (30); R. Paternoster (26)
JQC	R.J. Sampson (75); D.S. Nagin (38); D.P. Farrington (33); D.L. Weisburd (33); S.W. Raudenbush (32)
JRCD	R.J. Sampson (66); S.W. Raudenbush (25); T.E. Moffitt (24); D.P. Farrington (18); J.H. Laub (17)
JIV	M.A. Straus (90); M.P. Koss (57); J.C. Campbell (47); K.D. O'Leary (39); M. Testa (31)
VAV	M.A. Straus (60); R. Caetano (25); V.A. Foshee (22); K.D. O'Leary (22); M.P. Koss (20)

American criminal justice journals

JQ	R.L. Akers (28); R. Tewksbury (28); D.J. Steffensmeier (25); J.H. Kramer (23); R.J. Sampson (20)
JCJ	F.T. Cullen (154); R.J. Sampson (101); A.R. Piquero (95); D.P. Farrington (58); T. Hirschi (54)
CAD	F.T. Cullen (26); R.J. Sampson (21); J.T. Ulmer (20); R. Paternoster (19); R. Loeber (18); A.R. Piquero (18)
CJR	F.T. Cullen (18); C.C. Spohn (16); D.J. Steffensmeier (16); D. Finkelhor (10); K.J. Mitchell (10); D.W. Osgood (10); A.R. Piquero (10)
FP	D.A. Andrews (15); P. Gendreau (9); J.L. Bonta (7); S. Covington (6); F.T. Cullen (6); M.L. Prendergast (6)

International criminology journals

ANZ	R.J. Sampson (20); C. Cunneen (13); D. Indermauer (12); D.S. Nagin (11); R. Paternoster (11)
BJC	D. Garland (17); R. Reiner (17); T.R. Tyler (17); I. Loader (16); T. Jefferson (15)
CJC	D. Bigo (7); R.J.R. Blair (6); R.V. Ericson (6); M. Foucault (6); D. Garland (6); G. Gudjonsson (6); C.D. Shearing (6); T.R. Tyler (6)
CLSC	J. Young (23); W.S. DeKeseredy (21); R.A. Matthews (16); M.D. Schwartz (16); C.W. Mullins (14)
CRGE	M. Parazelli (17); S. Brochu (9); M. Landry (8); F. Vitaro (8)

International criminal justice journals

CAJ	R.J. Sampson (22); D.L. Weisburd (17); W.G. Skogan (16); E.R. Maguire (13); G.L. Kelling (12)
CJB	J.L. Bonta (41); R.K. Hanson (40); R.D. Hare (39); A.R. Piquero (39); D.P. Farrington (35)
IJCA	M. Rokeach (9); J.S. Goldkamp (8); E.A. Lind (7); S.H. Schwartz (6); J. Zhao (6)
IJOT	R.K. Hanson (43); W.L. Marshall (41); T.E. Moffitt (24); T. Ward (24); F.T. Cullen (23); R.D. Hare (23)
SJ	A. Davis (6); H. Gusterson (5); R.A. Leo (5); D.H. Price (5); A. Smith (5); D. Spade (5)

Note: For abbreviations of journals, see Table 5.1. The 5 most-cited scholars are shown in general, but there can be more or less than 5 in cases of ties

5.3 Most-Cited Scholars in Five Journals

was given a score of 25 and the next-most-cited scholar, Daniel S. Nagin, was given a score of 24. The next 2 scholars, David P. Farrington and David L. Weisburd, who were each ranked 3.5 because they were tied, were each given a score of 22.5. The ranking continued up to the 2 scholars with 13 citations, who were each ranked 24.5 and given a score of 1.5. A total of 25 scholars were given a score in JQC; all other scholars cited in this journal were scored 0. This procedure was originally developed as a way of equally weighting all the journals (Cohn & Farrington, 1994b). If the raw numbers of citations of each scholar in each journal had simply been added together, journals with a large number of citations (e.g., JCJ) would have contributed disproportionately to the total score.

Table 5.3 shows the 10 most-cited scholars in each group of 5 journals in 2010 and their comparative rankings (up to 30) in 2005, 2000, 1995, and 1990. The total score in 2010 is shown in the right-hand column. Robert J. Sampson was the most-cited scholar in American criminology journals in 2010, 2005, and 2000, compared with Travis Hirschi in 1995 and Marvin E. Wolfgang in 1990. Francis T. Cullen was the most-cited scholar in American criminal justice journals in 2010, compared with Robert J. Sampson in 2005, Francis T. Cullen again in 2000, Lawrence W. Sherman in 1995, and Joan Petersilia in 1990. David Garland was the most-cited scholar in international criminology journals in 2010, compared with David P. Farrington in 2005 and John Braithwaite in 2000, 1995, and 1990. R. Karl Hanson was the most-cited scholar in international criminal justice journals in 2010, compared with Robert J. Sampson in 2005, Robert D. Hare in 2000, Steven F. Messner in 1995, and Travis Hirschi in 1990.

In American criminology journals, only 1 of the top 10 scholars (Terrie E. Moffitt) was highly cited (among the top 25) in more than 3 of the 5 journals (all except JIV). Five of the top 10 scholars were highly cited in CRIM, JQC, and JRCD, and 1 (Alex R. Piquero) was highly cited in JQC and JRCD but not in CRIM. The other 3 (Murray A. Straus, Mary P. Koss, and K. Daniel O'Leary) were highly cited only in JIV and VAV. This clearly shows the effect of including these 2 more specialized journals. Francis T. Cullen was highly cited in all 5 American criminal justice journals, and the next 3 scholars were highly cited in 4 of the 5 journals (all except FP). David Garland was highly cited in 4 of the 5 international criminology journals, Robert J. Sampson and Michel Foucault were highly cited in 3 journals, and the remainder were highly cited in only 2 journals. In international criminal justice journals, the top 3 scholars and Robert J. Sampson were highly cited in 3 of the 5 journals (CAJ, CJB, and IJOT) and the other 6 scholars were highly cited in only 2 journals (CJB and IJOT). None of the 10 most-cited scholars in international criminal justice journals were highly cited in either IJCA or SJ.

In American criminology journals, 9 of the top 10 scholars in 2010 had also been in the top 30 in 2005, and 8 had been in the top 30 in 2000. The highest new entrants in 2010 were Stephen W. Raudenbush (2) and Jeffrey D. Morenoff (12). The highest-ranked scholars in 2005 who were not in the top 30 in 2010 were Michael R. Gottfredson (ranked 7 in 2005) and David Finkelhor (13.5). Three scholars were among the top 11 in all 5 years (Robert J. Sampson, David P. Farrington, and Murray

Table 5.3 Most-cited scholars in groups of five journals in 2010

Scholar	Rank in 2010	Rank in 2005	Rank in 2000	Rank in 1995	Rank in 1990	Score in 2010
Five American criminology journals						
Robert J. Sampson	1	1	1	5	10.5	75
Stephen W. Raudenbush	2	–	–	–	–	69
John H. Laub	3	2	5	21	–	62.5
Daniel S. Nagin	4	10	11.5	–	–	57
David P. Farrington	5	5	2	4	6.5	52.5
Terrie E. Moffitt	6	4	4	–	–	50.5
Murray A. Straus	7	6	6	2	6.5	50
Mary P. Koss	8	12	11.5	8	–	45
K. Daniel O'Leary	9	10	8	24.5	–	44.5
Alex R. Piquero	10	21.5	–	–	–	37.5
Five American criminal justice journals						
Francis T. Cullen	1	2	1	12.5	14	112
Robert J. Sampson	2	1	4	–	–	84
Alex R. Piquero	3.5	6	–	–	–	72.5
Darrell J. Steffensmeier	3.5	22	–	–	–	72.5
Raymond Paternoster	5.5	14.5	–	–	–	46
Cassia C. Spohn	5.5	7.5	–	–	–	46
Jeffrey T. Ulmer	7	7.5	–	–	–	42
John H. Kramer	8	–	–	–	–	41
Michael R. Gottfredson	9	–	–	4	20	40.5
Travis Hirschi	10	16.5	6	2	5.5	40
Five international criminology journals						
David Garland	1	6	6	–	–	59.5
Tom R. Tyler	2	–	–	–	–	45
Robert J. Sampson	3	–	23.5	–	–	44
Michel Foucault	4	–	2	27	–	38.5
Richard V. Ericson	5	–	3	20.5	7.5	37
John H. Laub	6	–	–	–	–	31.5
Daniel S. Nagin	7	–	–	–	–	30
Alex R. Piquero	8	–	–	–	–	29.5
Jock Young	9	24.5	9	20.5	–	27
Five international criminal justice journals						
R. Karl Hanson	1	12	–	–	–	63.5
Marnie E. Rice	2	5	18.5	–	–	50
Grant T. Harris	3	11	18.5	–	–	45.5
Robert D. Hare	4	6	1	18.5	6	43
Terrie E. Moffitt	5	–	5	–	–	42.5
Robert J. Sampson	6	1	–	5	–	41
James L. Bonta	7	2	28.5	–	–	37.5
Alex R. Piquero	8	–	–	–	–	36
Francis T. Cullen	9	18.5	22	22.5	26.5	36
Jill S. Levenson	10	–	–	–	–	32

Note: Fewer than 10 scholars are shown where there are ties. Ranks up to 30 in prior years are shown

A. Straus). Of the top 7 scholars in 1990, only David P. Farrington and Murray A. Straus survived to be in the 10 most-cited scholars in 2010.

In American criminal justice journals, 8 of the top 10 scholars in 2010 had been in the top 30 in 2005, but only 3 had been in the top 30 in 2000. The highest new entrants were John H. Kramer (8) and Richard Tewksbury (11.5). Francis T. Cullen and Travis Hirschi were among the top 17 scholars in all 5 years. The highest-ranked scholars in 2005 who were not in the top 30 in 2010 were Harold G. Grasmick (ranked 5 in 2005) and Robert E. Worden (9). Only Travis Hirschi of the top 6 scholars in 1990 survived to be in the top 10 scholars in 2010.

In international criminology journals, only 2 of the top 9 scholars in 2010 had been in the top 30 in 2005, although 5 had been in the top 30 in 2000. Four were new entrants; the highest new entrants were Tom R. Tyler (2) and John H. Laub (6). None were among the top 25 scholars in all 5 years, although Richard V. Ericson and Jock Young were among the top 25 scholars in 4 years. The highest-ranked scholars in 2005 who were not in the top 30 in 2010 were Lawrence W. Sherman (ranked 3 in 2005) and Michael Levi (4). Only 1 of the top 8 scholars in 1990 was among the top 10 scholars in 2010: Richard V. Ericson. Given the big change in the most-cited scholars between 2005 and 2010, it seems likely that the main focus of some of the international criminology journals may have changed considerably between 2005 and 2010.

In international criminal justice journals, 7 of the top 10 scholars in 2010 had been in the top 30 in 2005, and 6 had been in the top 30 in 2000. Robert D. Hare and Francis T. Cullen were among the top 30 scholars in all 5 years. The highest new entrants in 2010 were Alex R. Piquero (8) and Jill S. Levenson (10). The highest-ranked scholars in 2005 who were not in the top 30 in 2010 were John H. Laub (ranked 4 in 2005) and Lawrence E. Cohen (7). Only Robert D. Hare of the top 6 scholars in 1990 survived to be in the top 10 scholars in 2010.

5.4 Most-Cited Scholars in Ten Journals

Table 5.4 shows the 10 most-cited scholars in each group of 10 journals in 2010 and their comparative rankings (up to 30) in 2005, 2000, 1995, and 1990. The total score in 2010 is shown in the right-hand column. Robert J. Sampson was the most-cited scholar in criminology journals, as he had been in 2000, compared with David P. Farrington in 2005, Travis Hirschi in 1995, and Marvin E. Wolfgang in 1990. Francis T. Cullen was the most-cited scholar in criminal justice journals in 2010, as he had been in 2000, compared with Robert J. Sampson in 2005, Lawrence W. Sherman in 1995, and Travis Hirschi in 1990. Robert J. Sampson was most-cited in American journals in 2010, as he had been in 2005 and 2000, compared with Travis Hirschi in 1995 and Marvin E. Wolfgang in 1990. Robert J. Sampson was also most-cited in international journals in 2010, compared with David P. Farrington in 2005, John Braithwaite in 2000, Lawrence W. Sherman in 1995, and Francis T. Cullen in 1990.

Table 5.4 Most-cited scholars in groups of ten journals in 2010

Scholar	Rank in 2010	Rank in 2005	Rank in 2000	Rank in 1995	Rank in 1990	Score in 2010
Ten criminology journals						
Robert J. Sampson	1	2	1	8.5	24.5	119
John H. Laub	2	4	8	28	–	94
Daniel S. Nagin	3	6	20.5	–	–	87
David P. Farrington	4	1	2	3	3	74
Stephen W. Raudenbush	5	–	–	–	–	69.5
Alex R. Piquero	6	–	–	–	–	67
David Garland	7	20	12	–	–	59.5
Terrie E. Moffitt	8	3	7	–	–	50.5
Murray A. Straus	9	8.5	9	2	10	50
Alfred Blumstein	10	23	–	11	4	45.5
Ten criminal justice journals						
Francis T. Cullen	1	2	1	4	11	148
Robert J. Sampson	2	1	4	10	–	125
Alex R. Piquero	3	13.5	–	–	–	108.5
R. Karl Hanson	4	24.5	–	–	–	77.5
Darrell J. Steffensmeier	5	–	–	–	–	72.5
David P. Farrington	6	13.5	5	27	4	71
Terrie E. Moffitt	7.5	–	6.5	–	–	62.5
Cassia C. Spohn	7.5	16.5	–	–	–	62.5
James L. Bonta	9	4	–	–	–	60.5
Don A. Andrews	10	5	15	12	–	56.5
Ten American journals						
Robert J. Sampson	1	1	1	6	18	159
Francis T. Cullen	2	5	8.5	29	26.5	133.5
Alex R. Piquero	3	10	–	–	–	110
David P. Farrington	4	4	3	8	5	92
Darrell J. Steffensmeier	5	26	–	–	–	91
Daniel S. Nagin	6	9	18.5	–	–	90
John H. Laub	7	2	8.5	30	–	88
Stephen W. Raudenbush	8	–	–	–	–	81.5
Terrie E. Moffitt	9	6	4	–	–	70.5
Raymond Paternoster	10	8	22	–	–	67
Ten international journals						
Robert J. Sampson	1	2	15	–	–	85
R. Karl Hanson	2	21	–	–	–	80.5
Alex R. Piquero	3	–	–	–	–	65.5
David Garland	4	5	3	–	–	59.5
Michel Foucault	5	–	2	–	24	54.5
David P. Farrington	6	1	19	6	6.5	53
Marnie E. Rice	7	14.5	–	–	–	50
Tom R. Tyler	8	–	–	–	–	48.5
Grant T. Harris	9.5	20	–	–	–	45.5
Daniel S. Nagin	9.5	–	–	–	–	45.5

Note: Ranks up to 30 in prior years are shown

In criminology journals, 8 of the top 10 scholars in 2010 had been in the top 30 in 2005, compared with 7 in 2000. The highest-ranked scholars in 2005 who were not in the top 30 in 2010 were Clifford D. Shearing (ranked 7 in 2005) and Lawrence W. Sherman (8.5). Of those in the top 10 in 2010, Robert J. Sampson, David P. Farrington, and Murray A. Straus were in the top 30 scholars in all 5 years. The highest new entrants in 2010 were Stephen W. Raudenbush (4) and Alex R. Piquero (5). Only 2 of the top 5 scholars in 1990 survived to be in the top 10 scholars in 2010: David P. Farrington and Alfred Blumstein.

In criminal justice journals, 8 of the top 10 scholars in 2010 had been in the top 30 in 2005, compared with 5 in 2000. The highest-ranked scholars in 2005 who were not in the top 30 in 2010 were Joan Petersilia (ranked 7 in 2005), Harold G. Grasmick (8), and Robert J. Bursik (9). Of the top 10 scholars in 2010, Francis T. Cullen and David P. Farrington were in the top 30 scholars in all 5 years. The highest new entrants in 2010 were Darrell J. Steffensmeier (5) and Daniel S. Nagin (14). Only 1 of the top 5 scholars in 1990 survived to be in the top 10 in 2010: David P. Farrington.

In American journals, 9 of the top 10 scholars in 2010 had been in the top 30 in 2005, and 7 were in the top 30 in 2000. The highest-ranked scholars in 2005 who were not in the top 30 in 2010 were Harold G. Grasmick (ranked 11 in 2005) and Richard J. Gelles (15.5). Three of the top 10 scholars in 2010 (Robert J. Sampson, Francis T. Cullen, and David P. Farrington) were in the top 30 in all 5 years. The highest new entrants in 2010 were Stephen W. Raudenbush (8) and John H. Kramer (18). Of the top 5 scholars in 1990, only David P. Farrington survived to be in the top 10 scholars in 2010.

In international journals, 6 of the top 10 scholars in 2010 had been in the top 30 in 2005, compared with 4 in 2000. The highest-ranked scholars in 2005 who were not in the top 30 in 2010 were John Braithwaite (ranked 4 in 2005), Lawrence W. Sherman (6), and Clifford D. Shearing (9.5). Of the top 10 scholars in 2010, only 1 (David P. Farrington) was in the top 30 in all 5 years. The highest new entrants in 2010 were Alex R. Piquero (3) and Tom R. Tyler (8). Only 1 of the top 7 scholars in 1990 survived to be in the top 10 in 2010: David P. Farrington.

5.5 Most-Cited Scholars in 20 Journals

Table 5.5 shows the 39 most-cited scholars in all 20 journals in 2010 and their comparative rankings (up to 40) in 2005, 2000, 1995, and 1990. The most-cited scholar in 2010, as in 2005 and 2000, was Robert J. Sampson, compared with Lawrence W. Sherman in 1995 and Marvin E. Wolfgang in 1990. Sampson advanced from 38 in 1990 to 5 in 1995 and first in 2000. Between 2005 and 2010, big advances were made by Alex R. Piquero (from 16 to 2) and Rolf Loeber (from 29.5 to 17). Moving downwards were James L. Bonta (from 5 to 18) and Don A. Andrews (from 9 to 22).

The comparison of citation rankings over the years shows the advance of a new generation of scholars such as Sampson and John H. Laub (and even younger

Table 5.5 Most-cited scholars in all 20 journals in 2010

Rank in 2010	Rank in 2005	Rank in 2000	Rank in 1995	Rank in 1990	Name	CRM score	CJ score	Total
1	1	1	5	38	Robert J. Sampson	119	125	244
2	16	–	–	–	Alex R. Piquero	67	108.5	175.5
3	4	3	18	7	Francis T. Cullen	21.5	148	169.5
4	3	2	4	3	David P. Farrington	74	71	145
5	8	–	–	–	Daniel S. Nagin	87	48.5	135.5
6	2	13.5	–	–	John H. Laub	94	36.5	119.5
7	7	5	–	–	Terrie E. Moffitt	50.5	62.5	113
8	–	–	–	–	Stephen W. Raudenbush	69.5	32.5	102
9	–	–	–	–	R. Karl Hanson	17	77.5	94.5
10	–	–	–	–	Darrell J. Steffensmeier	18.5	72.5	91
11	13	23.5	–	–	Raymond Paternoster	42.5	46	88.5
12	6	4	2	2	Travis Hirschi	29.5	52	81.5
13	–	–	–	–	Wesley G. Skogan	19.5	52	71.5
14	–	8	24	–	Michel Foucault	38.5	28.5	67
15	–	–	–	–	David L. Weisburd	34	32.5	66.5
16	–	–	–	–	Cassia C. Spohn	0	62.5	62.5
17	29.5	17	–	35	Rolf Loeber	35	26	61
18	5	31	–	–	James L. Bonta	0	60.5	60.5
19	14	9	–	–	David Garland	59.5	0	59.5
20	11	27.5	3	5	Michael R. Gottfredson	11.5	47	58.5
21	–	–	–	–	Jeffrey T. Ulmer	15	42	57
22	9	35.5	20	–	Don A. Andrews	0	56.5	56.5
23	–	–	26	4	Alfred Blumstein	45.5	8	53.5
24	–	–	–	–	Ronald C. Kramer	20	32.5	52.5
25.5	21	15	6	10.5	Murray A. Straus	50	0	50
25.5	33	–	–	–	Marnie E. Rice	0	50	50
27	–	–	–	–	Tom R. Tyler	45	4	49
28	15	21	–	21.5	Paul Gendreau	0	47	47
29	–	–	–	–	Grant T. Harris	0	45.5	45.5
30	35.5	–	10	–	Mary P. Koss	45	0	45
31	33	27.5	–	–	K. Daniel O'Leary	44.5	0	44.5
32	17	20	–	–	Robert D. Hare	0	43	43
33	–	–	–	–	John H. Kramer	0	41	41
34	–	–	–	–	Richard Tewksbury	0	40	40
35	–	–	–	–	Ronald L. Akers	0	39	39
36	–	16	38	39	Richard V. Ericson	37	0	37
37	–	–	–	–	Jeffrey D. Morenoff	34.5	0	34.5
38.5	38	–	–	–	Avshalom Caspi	32.5	0	32.5
38.5	–	23.5	–	–	Stanley Cohen	16.5	16	32.5

Note: Ranks up to 40 in prior years are shown

5.5 Most-Cited Scholars in 20 Journals

Table 5.6 Comparison of 20 journals in 2010 and 9 journals in 2006–2010

20 journals in 2010		Nine journals in 2006–2010	
Rank	Scholar	Rank	Scholar
1	Robert J. Sampson	1	Robert J. Sampson
2	Alex R. Piquero	2	David P. Farrington
3	Francis T. Cullen	3	Alex R. Piquero
4	David P. Farrington	4	Francis T. Cullen
5	Daniel S. Nagin	5	John H. Laub
6	John H. Laub	6	Terrie E. Moffitt
7	Terrie E. Moffitt	7	Travis Hirschi
8	Stephen W. Raudenbush	8	Raymond Paternoster
9	R. Karl Hanson	9	Daniel S. Nagin
10	Darrell J. Steffensmeier	10	Michael R. Gottfredson
11	Raymond Paternoster	11	Alfred Blumstein
12	Travis Hirschi	12	Stephen W. Raudenbush
13	Wesley G. Skogan	13	Rolf Loeber
14	Michel Foucault	14	Darrell J. Steffensmeier
15	David L. Weisburd	15	Lawrence W. Sherman
16	Cassia C. Spohn	16.5	Robert Brame
17	Rolf Loeber	16.5	Tom R. Tyler
18	James L. Bonta	18	Robert J. Bursik
19	David Garland	19	Robert Agnew
20	Michael R. Gottfredson	20	Harold G. Grasmick

scholars such as Piquero) and the corresponding decline of older (and deceased) scholars such as Wolfgang and Michael J. Hindelang. David P. Farrington is notable for the unusual stability of his rankings over the 5 time periods (ranked 3 in 1990, 4 in 1995, 2 in 2000, 3 in 2005, and 4 in 2010). Travis Hirschi is also fairly stable, although there appears to be a downward trend (he was ranked 2 in 1990 and 1995, 4 in 2000, 6 in 2005, and 12 in 2010). The top 7 scholars in 2010 had been in the top 40 in 2005; the highest new entrants were Stephen W. Raudenbush (8), R. Karl Hanson (9), and Darrell J. Steffensmeier (10). Conversely, 9 of the top 10 scholars in 2005 were still in the top 40 in 2010. The highest-ranked scholars in 2005 who were not in the top 40 in 2010 were Lawrence W. Sherman (ranked 10 in 2005) and John Braithwaite (12).

Three of the 10 most-cited scholars in 2010 (Daniel S. Nagin, John H. Laub, and Stephen W. Raudenbush) were more highly cited in criminology journals than in criminal justice journals. Five (Alex R. Piquero, Francis T. Cullen, Terrie E. Moffitt, R. Karl Hanson, Darrell J. Steffensmeier) were more highly cited in criminal justice journals. Robert J. Sampson and David P. Farrington were about equally cited in both types of journals. This was a change from earlier years, when most of the top 10 scholars were more highly cited in criminology journals.

Table 5.6 compares the results obtained from 20 journals in 1 year with those obtained from 9 journals in 5 years and shows that there was a considerable overlap of the most-cited scholars. Thirteen of the 20 most-cited scholars in 20 journals in

2010 were among the 20 most-cited scholars in 9 journals in 2006–2010. However, it was noticeable that 5 of the more international scholars on the 20-journal list (James L. Bonta, Michel Foucault, David Garland, R. Karl Hanson, David L. Weisburd) were missing from the top 20 on the 9-journal list, most likely because the 9-journal list gave less weight to international journals. Nineteen of the top 20 scholars on the 20-journal list (all except Wesley G. Skogan) were in the top 50 on the 9-journal list, an impressive level of agreement. This is not surprising, because the 9 journals were included in the 20 journals and 2010 is included in 2006–2010. Nevertheless, it is clear that international scholars such as James L. Bonta and R. Karl Hanson, and scholars in less mainstream areas such as Murray A. Straus and Mary P. Koss, tend to be given higher rankings in the 20-journal analysis than in the 9-journal analysis.

5.6 Further Analyses

Table 5.7 shows the 2 most-cited works of the 10 most-cited scholars in all 20 journals in 2010. The most-cited works of the most-cited scholar, Robert J. Sampson, were "Neighborhoods and violent crime" (Sampson, Raudenbush, & Earls, 1997) and *Crime in the Making* (Sampson & Laub, 1993). The number of Sampson's citations of this latter work differed from those of John H. Laub because of the exclusion of self-citations. Unlike previous years, the majority of the most-cited works of the 10 most-cited scholars in 2010 were journal articles or book chapters (13) rather than books (7). The 2 most-cited works of Sampson, Laub, and Moffitt were the same as in 2005. One of the 2 most-cited works of Cullen ("The empirical status of Gottfredson and Hirschi's general theory of crime": Pratt & Cullen, 2000) and Farrington ("The criminal career paradigm": Piquero, Farrington, & Blumstein, 2003) were the same as in 2005. Most of these works were concerned with longitudinal/criminal career research and/or theories. However, there are now more works on methodology and meta-analysis.

Table 5.8 shows the total number of citations of the 10 most-cited scholars in 2010, together with the number of different articles in which they were cited (prevalence), and the average number of citations per article (frequency). Because of the scoring system which gave equal weight to each journal, some authors with high scores (e.g., R. Karl Hanson and Darrell J. Steffensmeier) had fewer citations than others; they were highly cited in journals that contained relatively few citations.

As an example, John H. Laub had 187 total citations and was cited in 93 different articles. His average number of citations per article was therefore 2.0. A high frequency of citations per article, or being cited many times in a few articles, may be a poorer measure of influence on a large number of other scholars than a high prevalence of citations. R. Karl Hanson and Darrell J. Steffensmeier had a relatively high frequency of citations combined with a relatively low prevalence, so they had a high number of citations per article. Counting the total number of citations may overestimate the influence of these scholars and underestimate the influence of scholars

5.6 Further Analyses

Table 5.7 Most-cited works of the most-cited scholars in 2010

Rank	Author/work	Number of citations
1	Robert J. Sampson (90 different works cited)	
	Sampson, R. J., Raudenbush, S. W., & Earls, F. E. (1997). Neighborhoods and violent crime: A multilevel study of collective efficacy. *Science, 277*, 918–924.	50
	Sampson, R. J., & Laub, J. H. (1993). *Crime in the making.* Cambridge, MA: Harvard University Press.	39
2	Alex R. Piquero (120 different works cited)	
	Paternoster, R., Brame, R., Mazerolle, P. J., & Piquero, A. R. (1998). Using the correct statistical test for the equality of regression coefficients. *Criminology, 36*, 859–866.	23
	Piquero, A. R., Farrington, D. P., & Blumstein, A. (2003). The criminal career paradigm. In M. Tonry (Ed.) *Crime and justice* (Vol. 30, pp. 359–506). Chicago: University of Chicago Press.	14
3	Francis T. Cullen (119 different works cited)	
	Pratt, T. C., & Cullen, F. T. (2000). The empirical status of Gottfredson and Hirschi's general theory of crime: A meta-analysis. *Criminology, 38*, 931–964.	35
	Cullen, F. T., Fisher, B. S., & Applegate, B. K. (2000). Public opinion about punishment and corrections. In M. Tonry (Ed.), *Crime and justice* (Vol. 27, pp. 1–79). Chicago: University of Chicago Press.	12
4	David P. Farrington (128 different works cited)	
	Piquero, A. R., Farrington, D. P., & Blumstein, A. (2003). The criminal career paradigm. In M. Tonry (Ed.), *Crime and justice* (Vol. 30, pp. 359–506). Chicago: University of Chicago Press.	21
	Piquero, A. R., Farrington, D. P., & Blumstein, A. (2007). *Key issues in criminal career research.* Cambridge, UK: Cambridge University Press.	14
5	Daniel S. Nagin (64 different works cited)	
	Nagin, D. S. (2005). *Group-based modeling of development.* Cambridge, MA: Harvard University Press.	20
	Nagin, D. S. (1999). Analyzing developmental trajectories: A semi-parametric group-based approach. *Psychological Methods, 4*, 139–157.	14
6	John H. Laub (42 different works cited)	
	Sampson, R. J., & Laub, J. H. (1993). *Crime in the making.* Cambridge, MA: Harvard University Press.	38
	Laub, J. H., & Sampson, R. J. (2003). *Shared beginnings, divergent lives.* Cambridge, MA: Harvard University Press.	24
7	Terrie E. Moffitt (72 different works cited)	
	Moffitt, T. E. (1993). Adolescence-limited and life-course-persistent antisocial behavior: A developmental taxonomy. *Psychological Review, 100*, 674–701.	44
	Moffitt, T. E, Caspi, A., Rutter, M., & Silva, P. A. (2001). *Sex differences in antisocial behaviour.* Cambridge, UK: Cambridge University Press.	10

(continued)

Table 5.7 (continued)

Rank	Author/work	Number of citations
8	Stephen W. Raudenbush (25 different works cited)	
	Sampson, R. J., Raudenbush, S. W., & Earls, F. E. (1997). Neighborhoods and violent crime: A multilevel study of collective efficacy. *Science*, *277*, 918–924.	50
	Raudenbush, S. W., & Bryk, A. S. (2002). *Hierarchical linear models*. Thousand Oaks, CA: Sage. (Multiple editions)	34
9	R. Karl Hanson (38 different works cited)	
	Hanson, R. K., & Bussière, M. T. (1998). Predicting relapse: A meta-analysis of sexual offender recidivism studies. *Journal of Consulting and Clinical Psychology*, *61*, 646–652.	16
	Hanson, R. K., & Morton-Bourgon, K. E. (2005). The characteristics of persistent sexual offenders: A meta-analysis of recidivism studies. *Journal of Consulting and Clinical Psychology*, *73*, 1154–1163.	12
10	Darrell J. Steffensmeier (32 different works cited)	
	Steffensmeier, D. J., Ulmer, J. T., & Kramer, J. (1998). The interaction of race, gender, and age in criminal sentencing: The punishment cost of being young, black, and male. *Criminology*, *36*, 763–798.	23
	Steffensmeier, D. J., & Demuth, S. (2000). Ethnicity and sentencing outcomes in U.S. federal courts: Who is punished more harshly? *American Sociological Review*, *65*, 705–729.	16

Table 5.8 Prevalence, frequency, specialization, and versatility

Rank	Author	Total citations	No. different articles[a]	Citations/ article	No. different works[b]	Citations/ work	% Top 2[c]
1	Robert J. Sampson	495	178	2.78	90	5.50	18.0
2	Alex R. Piquero	278	136	2.04	120	2.32	14.9
3	Francis T. Cullen	334	157	2.13	119	2.81	11.1
4	David P. Farrington	248	111	2.23	128	1.94	14.1
5	Daniel S. Nagin	229	109	2.10	64	3.58	14.8
6	John H. Laub	187	93	2.01	42	4.45	33.2
7	Terrie E. Moffitt	216	99	2.18	72	3.00	25.0
8	Stephen W. Raudenbush	186	101	1.84	25	7.44	45.2
9	R. Karl Hanson	131	43	3.05	38	3.45	21.4
10	Darrell J. Steffensmeier	143	49	2.92	32	4.47	27.3

[a]This refers to the number of different articles in the 20 journals in which the author was cited
[b]This refers to the number of different works by the author that were cited in the 20 journals
[c]This refers to the percentage of total citations accounted for by the author's 2 most-cited works

with a high prevalence but not such a high frequency, such as Stephen W. Raudenbush, who have a lower number of citations per article. The total number of citations, however, is the most widely used measure. Robert J. Sampson had both a high prevalence and a high frequency.

The total number of citations can also be disaggregated into the number of different works cited and the average number of citations per work. Some scholars (defined above as versatile) may be highly cited primarily because they have a large number of different works cited, while others (defined above as specialized) may be highly cited because a small number of works are each cited many times. Table 5.8 shows 3 measures of specialization or versatility: the number of different works cited, the average number of citations per work, and the percentage of total citations accounted for by the 2 most-cited works. For example, Robert J. Sampson had a total of 495 citations of 90 different works, with an average of 5.5 citations per work. His 2 most-cited works accounted for 18 % of all his citations (89 out of 495).

On the criterion of the largest number of different works cited, David P. Farrington (128), Alex R. Piquero (120), and Francis T. Cullen (119) were the most versatile, whereas Stephen W. Raudenbush (25), Darrell J. Steffensmeier (32), and R. Karl Hanson (38) were the most specialized. On the criterion of the average number of citations per work, Stephen W. Raudenbush (7.4) and Robert J. Sampson (5.5) were the most specialized. Those with few citations per work were not necessarily versatile, because versatility depends also on the number of different works cited. Scholars with a low frequency of citations per work and a large number of different works cited (e.g., David P. Farrington, Alex R. Piquero, Francis T. Cullen) were the most versatile.

Stephen W. Raudenbush was the most specialized, in that 2 of his works accounted for a large fraction of all his citations. His 2 most-cited works accounted for 45 % of all his citations (84 out of 186). On this criterion, John H. Laub (33 %) and Darrell J. Steffensmeier (27 %) were also specialized, whereas Francis T. Cullen (11 %) and David P. Farrington (14 %) were the most versatile.

5.7 Conclusion

This study employs a longitudinal design in which citations are studied in the same set of 20 journals at 5-year intervals. Exactly the same methods and journals are used in each year. The nature of a longitudinal design results in several limitations. Because we are comparing results across years, we are unable to add new journals to the study but are limited to long-established journals that were being published at the time we began the research. Additionally, we cannot take advantage of new sources of citation data that have been developed but must use the same data collection method that was developed at the start of this research. However, the longitudinal design of this study is also a major strength. Studying the same set of journals at 5-year intervals allows us to examine citation trends over time and to consider how the influence of both scholars and works waxes and wanes.

Expanding the number of CCJ journals from 9 to 20 identified many of the same most-cited scholars found in other research that involved fewer journals. However, the rankings of some international scholars and some scholars working in less mainstream CCJ areas were improved when the number of journals was increased. The use of additional journals had both advantages and disadvantages. The obvious advantages of increased coverage were to some extent counteracted by the disadvantages of including progressively less mainstream CCJ journals. Continuing to expand the analysis to even more journals would require the inclusion of more peripheral or specialized journals, thus further diluting the importance of mainstream CCJ topics. It would, however, increase the visibility of scholars who publish in more specialized fields. The present results, like all citation analyses, depend to a considerable extent on the choice of journals that are analyzed.

The analysis of citations in 20 journals was restricted to data from only 1 year because this research was carried out with limited resources and no external funding. The use of only 1 year of citations in each journal inevitably caused more variability in the results over time than would occur in analyses based on 5 years. However, while the most-cited scholar in 1 journal could possibly be affected by 1 article that extensively cited a single author, the main focus of this paper is on identifying the most-cited scholars in groups of 5, 10, or 20 journals. Studying groups of journals, which are less vulnerable to such distortion, reduces the variability of the results and increases both the validity and reliability of the findings. Against the variability argument, there was considerable agreement between the results of this research and results obtained in earlier studies using the same set of journals, as well as results obtained using more years of data from smaller numbers of journals.

In order to make comparisons over time, this study focused primarily on the total number of citations as a method of determining scholarly influence but also reported prevalence (the number of different articles in which a scholar was cited) for the most-cited scholars. Prevalence may be a better measure of the influence of 1 scholar on others than raw citation counts. In addition, this research has shown the increasing citations of younger scholars and the decreasing citations of older scholars.

This research has identified some scholars (e.g., Stephen W. Raudenbush), as specialized, because their influence was based primarily on 1 or 2 highly cited works, mostly books. Other scholars (e.g., David P. Farrington, Francis T. Cullen) were versatile, because they had many different works, usually articles, that were cited only a few times each. Thus, it appears that there are 2 different ways in which scholarly influence operates in criminology and criminal justice. One way a scholar influences his or her colleagues is to write a scholarly book that proposes a new theory, such as *Crime in the Making* (Sampson & Laub, 1993); inevitably, the book is cited by later authors who discuss the theory. The second is to write a large number of different works on a variety of topics so that, while no individual work is a highly cited seminal work, the many articles that are "at risk" of being cited lead to a large number of total citations for the author.

This research also illustrates the possible importance of working with influential coauthors. For example, the most-cited scholar in the 20 journals in 2010 was

5.7 Conclusion

Robert J. Sampson; his second most-cited work was coauthored by John H. Laub, who was ranked sixth. In several tables in which Sampson is highly cited, Laub is also 1 of the most-cited scholars. This suggests that a scholar's influence may be related to the influence of his or her coauthors; publishing jointly with a scholar who publishes high-quality research and who publishes frequently may increase one's own prestige in the field.

While the study of 20 journals has both advantages and disadvantages in comparison with other analyses, these results add to the growing body of knowledge concerning changes in the most-cited and most influential scholars and works in criminology and criminal justice over time. Future research into citation analysis should continue this longitudinal series of studies and should focus more on changes in the most-cited works over time, perhaps as a way to eventually predict important research topics and provide greater assistance to policy makers. We conclude that these analyses reveal changes over time in scholarly influence and in theoretical concerns and policy issues.

Chapter 6
Conclusions

6.1 The Main Contribution of This Book

This book has documented the most-cited scholars in major criminology and criminal justice (CCJ) journals over a 25-year period as well as the most-cited works of the most-cited scholars. Successive analyses have tracked the most-cited scholars in 4 international journals, 6 American journals, and 20 American and international journals. These analyses show the waxing and waning of scholarly influence over time, as 1 generation ages and gives way to the next generation of scholars. They also reveal major trends over time, including the increasing number of cited authors and the increasing citations to articles rather than books.

Citation analysis is a valid measure of scholarly influence because it is highly correlated with other measures such as peer rankings, the receipt of academic prizes, and election to prestigious posts in scholarly societies. For example, of the most-cited 25 scholars in 20 journals in 2010, Robert J. Sampson, Francis T. Cullen, David P. Farrington, John H. Laub, Travis Hirschi, Daniel S. Nagin, and Alfred Blumstein have been President of the American Society of Criminology, and Robert J. Sampson, David P. Farrington, John H. Laub, Terrie E. Moffitt, and Alfred Blumstein have received the Stockholm Prize in Criminology.

Since we began our research in 1988, the use of citation analysis has enormously increased, largely because of the availability of Internet sources such as the Web of Science, Google Scholar, and Scopus. The journal impact factor, based on citations of articles 1–2 years after publication, has become enormously important and seems to be widely accepted as the main measure of the prestige of scholarly journals. And yet, as shown by the most-cited works of the most-cited scholars, this 1–2-year time window is much too short to capture most of the citations of CCJ works. As Cohn and Farrington (2012b) demonstrated, a highly cited CCJ article, such as "Adolescence-limited and life-course-persistent antisocial behavior" (Moffitt, 1993), may not become highly cited until at least 5–10 years after its publication.

Citation analyses that are based on Internet sources and carried out mechanically are inevitably unsatisfactory and full of errors, as we discussed in Chapter 1. Among the main problems are the inclusion of self-citations, the failure to correct errors in the original lists of references, the incorrect amalgamation of different persons with the same name and initials, and changes in coverage over time. Other problems include the fact that Google Scholar sets no standards for inclusion of material (presumably including everything on the Internet?) and provides no information about coverage.

The methods that we have used were carefully designed to overcome these problems. First, we have expended huge amounts of time to correct mistakes in reference lists, to distinguish different people with the same name and initials, to amalgamate the same people with different names, and to discover the scholars hidden by "et al." in reference lists. We were only able to do this because we have analyzed a limited number of the most prestigious journals in criminology and criminal justice and because of our personal knowledge of many scholars. Second, we eliminated all self-citations. Third, we analyzed the same journals over time, using exactly the same scoring methods that give equal weight to each journal, so that we could carry out longitudinal analyses of changes in the most-cited scholars over a 25-year time period. We believe that our citation analyses, although relatively limited in scope, produce more valid results than any citation analyses based on any Internet source. And we believe that our citation analyses provide valid information about changes over time in scholarly influence in criminology and criminal justice.

6.2 Policy Implications

An examination of the most-cited scholars and works indicates those topics that criminological researchers consider to be of most importance in different time periods. The most-cited works may also reflect current policy concerns, and an awareness of the topics that criminologists consider to be important and influential should guide policy makers and legislators in the development of new public policies.

In 20 journals, the most-cited works of 5 of the 6 most-cited scholars in 1990 focused on criminal career research (Cohn, Farrington, & Wright, 1998). This research should inform criminal justice decision making because it can provide useful information about the likely future course of criminal careers. The other most-cited scholar in 1990 was Travis Hirschi, and his most-cited work was the theoretical book *Causes of Delinquency* (Hirschi, 1969). According to Laub (2004, p. 18), "successful theories… provide influential guides to public policy." The main policy implication of this theory is that efforts should be made to increase individuals' bonding to society. The seventh most-cited scholar was Francis T. Cullen, and his most-cited work was *Reaffirming Rehabilitation* (Cullen & Gilbert, 1982), which has clear implications for effective correctional treatment. The eighth most-cited scholar was Ronald V. Clarke, and his most-cited work was *The Reasoning Criminal*

6.2 Policy Implications

(Cornish & Clarke, 1986). This book propounded a rational choice theory of offending that has important implications for situational crime prevention.

The most-cited works of the most-cited scholars in 1995 also had clear policy implications (Cohn & Farrington, 1999). *Policing Domestic Violence* (Sherman, 1992) was the most-cited work of the most-cited scholar, and this book reported research that encouraged police to arrest male domestic violence offenders. The most-cited work of the next 2 scholars was *A General Theory of Crime* (Gottfredson & Hirschi, 1990), which proposed that offending depended on self-control. A clear implication of this theory is that policy makers should develop early intervention programs to improve juveniles' self-control at a young age, perhaps focusing on parent training (Piquero, Jennings, & Farrington, 2010). The next most-cited work, *Understanding and Controlling Crime* (Farrington, Ohlin, & Wilson, 1986), set out methods of advancing knowledge about the development of criminal careers and how this knowledge might be used to reduce offending.

Similar policy implications can be drawn from the most-cited works of the most-cited scholars in 2000. The most-cited work of the most-cited scholar was *Crime in the Making* (Sampson & Laub, 1993), which reported on the development of offending and proposed that the most important theoretical construct was informal social control. The main implication of this theory is that bonding to the family, the school, and the community should be increased, through programs such as those providing job training and structured routine activities in adulthood. It also suggests that desistance can be encouraged by fostering bonding to adult institutions such as employment and marriage. Another suggestion is that informal social control in communities could be improved by increasing community cohesiveness or "collective efficacy" (Sampson, Raudenbush, & Earls, 1997). The theory also suggests that it is important to minimize labelling or stigmatization of offenders by reducing the use of incarceration.

Some of the other most-cited scholars in 2000 were the same as in earlier years: David P. Farrington for the development of offending, Francis T. Cullen for the effectiveness of correctional treatment, Travis Hirschi for the general theory of crime, and Lawrence W. Sherman for policing domestic violence. However, a new entry was *Crime, Shame, and Reintegration* by John Braithwaite (1989), with the policy implication of restorative justice programs for offenders.

Another new entry in 2000 was Terrie E. Moffitt's (1993) theory, which implies that different types of programs are needed for adolescence-limited and life-course-persistent offenders. For adolescence-limited offenders, it is especially important to limit contact with delinquent peers. Research on co-offending (Reiss & Farrington, 1991) suggests that it is essential to identify and target "recruiters," or offenders who repeatedly commit crimes with younger, less-experienced offenders, and who seem to be dragging increasing numbers of young people into crime. Programs that put antisocial peers together may have harmful effects (Dishion, McCord, & Poulin, 1999). Moffitt also suggests that, in order to target the "maturity gap" of adolescence-limited offenders, it is important to provide opportunities for them to achieve status and material goods by legitimate means.

The most-cited works of the most-cited scholars in 2005 show both continuity and change in their theoretical concerns and policy implications. The most-cited work of the most-cited scholar was still *Crime in the Making* (Sampson & Laub, 1993). The criminal career paradigm and developmental research were still important, as was rational choice theory, the effectiveness of correctional treatment, and the theories of Moffitt (1993) and of Gottfredson and Hirschi (1990). A newly identified work with clear policy implications for reducing crime was *Preventing Crime* by Lawrence W. Sherman and his colleagues (1997). *The Psychology of Criminal Conduct*, by Don A. Andrews and James L. Bonta (2003), was also identified as important, possibly because of its emphasis on the policy issues of risk assessment and correctional effectiveness.

Continuity and change is also evident in the most-cited works of the most-cited scholars in 2010. The most-cited scholar was still Robert J. Sampson, but his most-cited work was now "Neighborhoods and violent crime" (Sampson et al., 1997) with its policy implication of "collective efficacy" and increasing community cohesiveness. Perhaps because of the increasing importance of the Internet, the most-cited works were for the first time more likely to be articles rather than books. Another change was the increasing number of most-cited works that were primarily methodological rather than substantive: those of Alex R. Piquero (Paternoster, Brame, Mazerolle, & Piquero, 1998), Stephen W. Raudenbush (Raudenbush & Bryk, 2002), and Daniel S. Nagin (2005).

R. Karl Hanson was propelled into the top 10 because of his meta-analyses of sexual offender recidivism (Hanson & Bussière, 1998; Hanson & Morton-Bourgon, 2005). Another important topic with clear policy implications is racial bias in sentencing, which propelled Darrell J. Steffensmeier into the 10 most-cited scholars in 2010. However, the major topics of previous years—longitudinal and criminal career research and criminological theories—were still very much in evidence.

6.3 Future Citation Research

We hope that this book has demonstrated how much information the analysis of citations and publications has yielded about a wide variety of topics. The most pressing need in the future is for funding to carry out citation and publication analyses of larger numbers of journals and books in criminology and criminal justice. With funding, it would be possible to expand these analyses to later periods of time and to trace citation careers of scholars and works over long time periods. The aim should be to trace complete citation and publication trajectories of scholars, and citation trajectories of works, and to investigate to what extent the later trajectory can be predicted from the first few years. It is also important to investigate how long a scholar's influence persists after his or her death. We believe that it is useful to apply criminal career concepts such as onset, duration, termination, frequency, versatility, specialization, and escalation to the study of citation and publication careers. As we have shown, some scholars are highly cited because of 1 or 2 seminal works, whereas others are highly cited because of their large number of publications.

With funding, it would be possible to carry our more extensive analyses of the most-cited works of the most-cited scholars, to document changes over time in the most influential scholars and works in more detail, and also to identify highly cited works by less highly cited scholars. Ideally, vitae of the most influential scholars should be collected, so that all their publications, and citations of all their works, could be studied. It would also be important to relate the changing influence of scholars and works to changes in theoretical, empirical, methodological, and political concerns, and to the changing priorities of funding agencies. A crucial question is why certain scholars and topics (rather than others) become preeminent in certain time periods.

Further advances in the methodology of citation analysis are needed. In particular, the prevalence of citations (the number of different articles or books in which a work is cited) seems a more valid measure of influence than the more usual measure of the number of citations. In the interests of comparability over time, we had to keep measuring the number of citations. It would be desirable to develop a classification system for types of citations: whether they are favorable or unfavorable, to what extent they are perfunctory, how central to the argument they are, and so on. Measures of the number of words devoted to discussing a work, or the number of pages on which a work is cited, would also be useful. In addition, the prestige of citing and cited journals could be taken into account in inclusion criteria for citation analysis and in weighting citations. Also, the number and ordering of authors should be considered in citation analyses.

It is important to study the waxing and waning of scholarly influence over time. However, this requires using exactly the same methods and sources over time. This was a problem for us, as we could not include recently established influential journals such as *Criminology and Public Policy*, *Journal of Experimental Criminology*, or *European Journal of Criminology* in our citation analyses without reducing the comparability of our results over time.

In order to overcome problems of undesirable citation behavior (e.g., citing friends and departmental colleagues deliberately to boost their citations rather than because of their salience for the argument), research on citation behavior is needed. With funding, it would be possible to survey authors of books and journal articles to ask them why they cited certain scholars rather than others. It is important to investigate the extent to which authors obey the law of least effort and only read articles that are immediately available on the Internet, as opposed to books that have to be purchased or obtained from libraries. It is known that sales of scholarly books (other than textbooks) have declined greatly as the use of the Internet has increased (although this decline may be reversed as more e-books are published).

The effects of the specific interests of journal editors on the topics of articles published should be investigated. The types of works that are cited in a journal depend on the types of articles that are published in a journal. In turn, the selection of articles for publication depends on the editor, the editorial board, and referees. Editors can influence what is published by declining to review certain types of articles or by the choice of "easy" or "hard" referees. When an editor changes, there can be a marked change in the types of articles that are published and a corresponding marked change in the most-cited authors and most-cited works. It would be desirable for all journals to provide statistics on the number of articles submitted and accepted within different substantive categories, in order to investigate possible biases of editors and editorial boards.

A survey could include questions designed to investigate to what extent citation behavior is designed to curry favor with journal editors, likely reviewers, key staff members of funding agencies, and other individuals with power (e.g., heads of departments and presidents of scholarly societies). Systematic studies of similarities and dissimilarities between journals in topics covered and citations should be carried out. Research should investigate what types of articles in 1 journal tend to be cited in another journal (see Cohn & Farrington, 1990). In addition to eliminating self-citations, coauthor citations could be excluded from analyses, and even citations of scholars in the same department or the same university.

Overall, we believe that citation analysis is a very useful method of investigating changes in scholarly influence over time. However, funding is needed to transform it from its Cinderella status to an accepted discipline, to overcome future threats to its validity, and to establish it as a valuable method of documenting changes in influential scholars and topics in criminology and criminal justice over time.

References

Andrews, D. A., & Bonta, J. L. (1994). *The psychology of criminal conduct* (1st ed.). Cincinnati, OH: Anderson.
Andrews, D. A., & Bonta, J. L. (1998). *The psychology of criminal conduct* (2nd ed.). Cincinnati, OH: Anderson.
Andrews, D. A., & Bonta, J. L. (2003). *The psychology of criminal conduct* (3rd ed.). Cincinnati, OH: Anderson.
Andrews, D. A., Zinger, I., Hoge, R. D., Bonta, J. L., Gendreau, P., & Cullen, F. T. (1990). Does correctional treatment work? A clinically relevant and psychologically informed meta-analysis. *Criminology, 28*, 369–404.
Barbaree, H. E., & Marshall, W. L. (1989). Erectile responses among heterosexual child molesters, father-daughter incest offenders and matched nonoffenders: Five distinct age-preference profiles. *Canadian Journal of Behavioral Science, 21*, 70–82.
Barr, R., & Pease, K. (1990). Crime placement, displacement, and deflection. *Crime and Justice, 12*, 277–318.
Bauer, K., & Bakkalbasi, N. (2005). An examination of citation counts in a new scholarly communication environment. *D-Lib Magazine* [On-line serial], *11*(9). Retrieved April 24, 2013 from http://dlib.org/dlib/september05/bauer/09bauer.html
Bayley, D., & Shearing, C. D. (2001). *The new structure of policing*. Washington, DC: U.S. National Institute of Justice.
Blumstein, A., Cohen, J., & Farrington, D. P. (1988). Criminal career research: Its value for criminology. *Criminology, 26*, 1–35.
Blumstein, A., Cohen, J., Roth, J. A., & Visher, C. (Eds.). (1986). *Criminal careers and "career criminals". Vol. 1*. Washington, DC: National Academy Press.
Braithwaite, J. (1989). *Crime, shame, and reintegration*. Cambridge: Cambridge University Press.
Chapman, A. J. (1989). Assessing research: Citation-count shortcomings. *The Psychologist, 2*, 336–344.
Cohen, S. (1985). *Visions of social control: Crime, punishment, and classification*. Cambridge: Polity.
Cohen, L. E., & Felson, M. (1979). Social change and crime rate trends: A routine activity approach. *American Sociological Review, 44*, 588–608.
Cohn, E. G. (2009). Citation and content analysis. In J. M. Miller (Ed.), *21st century criminology: A reference handbook* (pp. 391–397). Thousand Oaks, CA: SAGE.
Cohn, E. G. (2011a). Changes in scholarly influence in major international criminology journals, 1986–2005. *Canadian Journal of Criminology and Criminal Justice, 53*, 157–188.
Cohn, E. G. (2011b). Changes in scholarly influence in major American criminology and criminal justice journals between 1986 and 2005. *Journal of Criminal Justice Education, 22*, 493–525.
Cohn, E. G., & Farrington, D. P. (1990). Differences between British and American criminology: An analysis of citations. *British Journal of Criminology, 30*, 467–482.

Cohn, E. G., & Farrington, D. P. (1994a). Who are the most influential criminologists in the English-speaking world? *British Journal of Criminology, 34*, 204–225.

Cohn, E. G., & Farrington, D. P. (1994b). Who are the most-cited scholars in major American criminology and criminal justice journals? *Journal of Criminal Justice, 22*, 517–534.

Cohn, E. G., & Farrington, D. P. (1995). The validity of citations as a measure of influence in criminology. *British Journal of Criminology, 35*, 143–145.

Cohn, E. G., & Farrington, D. P. (1996). Crime and justice and the criminology and criminal justice literature. *Crime and Justice: A Review of Research, 20*, 265–300.

Cohn, E. G., & Farrington, D. P. (1998a). Changes in the most-cited scholars in major international journals between 1986–90 and 1991–95. *British Journal of Criminology, 38*, 156–170.

Cohn, E. G., & Farrington, D. P. (1998b). Changes in the most-cited scholars in major American criminology and criminal justice journals between 1986–1990 and 1991–1995. *Journal of Criminal Justice, 26*, 99–116.

Cohn, E. G., & Farrington, D. P. (1998c). Assessing the quality of American doctoral program faculty in criminology and criminal justice, 1991–1995. *Journal of Criminal Justice Education, 9*, 187–210.

Cohn, E. G., & Farrington, D. P. (1999). Changes in the most-cited scholars in twenty criminology and criminal justice journals between 1990 and 1995. *Journal of Criminal Justice, 27*, 345–359.

Cohn, E. G., & Farrington, D. P. (2005). Citation research in criminology and criminal justice. In R. A. Wright & J. M. Miller (Eds.), *Encyclopedia of criminology* (pp. 176–177). New York, NY: Routledge.

Cohn, E. G., & Farrington, D. P. (2007a). Changes in scholarly influence in major international journals between 1986 and 2000. *Australian and New Zealand Journal of Criminology, 40*, 335–360.

Cohn, E. G., & Farrington, D. P. (2007b). Changes in scholarly influence in major American criminology and criminal justice journals between 1986 and 2000. *Journal of Criminal Justice Education, 18*, 6–34.

Cohn, E. G., & Farrington, D. P. (2008). Scholarly influence in criminology and criminal justice journals in 1990–2000. *Journal of Criminal Justice, 36*, 11–21.

Cohn, E. G., & Farrington, D. P. (2012a). Scholarly influence in criminology and criminal justice journals in 1990–2005. *Criminal Justice Review, 37*, 360–383.

Cohn, E. G., & Farrington, D. P. (2012b). *Scholarly influence in criminology and criminal justice.* New York, NY: Nova Science Publishers.

Cohn, E. G., Farrington, D. P., & Sorenson, J. R. (2000). Journal publications of Ph.D. graduates from American criminology and criminal justice programs, 1988–1997. *Journal of Criminal Justice Education, 11*, 35–49.

Cohn, E. G., Farrington, D. P., & Wright, R. A. (1998). *Evaluating criminology and criminal justice.* Westport, CT: Greenwood Press.

Cole, S. (1975). The growth of scientific knowledge: Theories of deviance as a case study. In L. A. Coser (Ed.), *The idea of social structure: Papers in honor of R.K. Merton* (pp. 175–200). New York, NY: Harcourt Brace Jovanovich.

Cole, J., & Cole, S. (1971). Measuring the quality of sociological research: Problems in the use of the Science Citation Index. *The American Sociologist, 6*, 23–29.

Cornish, D., & Clarke, R. V. (Eds.). (1986). *The reasoning criminal: Rational choice perspectives on offending.* New York, NY: Springer-Verlag.

Cullen, F. T. (2012). Foreword. In E. G. Cohn & D. P. Farrington (Eds.), *Scholarly productivity in criminology and criminal justice.* New York, NY: Nova Science Publishers (pp. vii–ix).

Cullen, F. T., Fisher, B. S., & Applegate, B. K. (2000). Public opinion about punishment and corrections. In M. Tonry (Ed.), *Crime and justice* (App, Vol. 27, pp. 1–79). Chicago, IL: University of Chicago Press.

Cullen, F. T., & Gilbert, K. E. (1982). *Reaffirming rehabilitation.* Cincinnati, OH: Anderson Publishing Co.

Cullen, F. T., Link, B. G., Wolfe, N. T., & Frank, J. (1985). The social dimensions of correctional officer stress. *Justice Quarterly, 2*, 503–533.

References

Davis, J., & Sorenson, J. R. (2010). Doctoral programs in criminal justice and criminology: A meta-analysis of program ranking. *Southwest Journal of Criminal Justice, 7*, 6–23.

Dess, H. M. 2006. Database reviews and reports: Scopus. *Issues in science and technology librarianship*, 45 (Winter). Retrieved April 24, 2013 from http://www.istl.org/06-winter/databases4.html.

DeZee, M. R. (1980). *The productivity of criminology and criminal justice faculty*. Chicago, IL: Joint Commission on Criminology and Criminal Justice Education and Standards.

Dishion, T. J., McCord, J., & Poulin, F. (1999). When interventions harm: Peer groups and problem behavior. *American Psychologist, 54*, 755–764.

Doob, A. N., & Roberts, J. V. (1983). *Sentencing: An analysis of the public's view*. Ottawa: Department of Justice.

Douglas, R. J. (1992). How to write a highly cited article without even trying. *Psychological Bulletin, 112*, 405–408.

Elliott, D. S., Huizinga, D. S., & Ageton, S. S. (1985). *Explaining delinquency and drug use*. Beverly Hills, CA: Sage Publications.

Ericson, R., & Haggerty, K. (1997). *Policing the risk society*. Oxford: Oxford University Press.

Fabianic, D. A. (1980). Perceived scholarship and readership of criminal justice journals. *Journal of Police Science and Administration, 8*, 15–20.

Fabianic, D. A. (1981). Institutional affiliation of authors in selected criminal justice journals. *Journal of Criminal Justice, 9*, 247–252.

Fabianic, D. A. (2001). Frequently published scholars and educational backgrounds. *Journal of Criminal Justice, 29*, 119–125.

Fabianic, D. A. (2002). Publication productivity of criminal justice faculty in criminal justice journals. *Journal of Criminal Justice, 30*, 549–558.

Fabianic, D. A. (2012). Publication profiles at point of promotion of criminal justice faculty. *Journal of Criminal Justice Education, 23*, 65–80.

Farrington, D. P. (1986). Age and crime. In M. Tonry & N. Morris (Eds.), *Crime and justice* (Vol. 7). Chicago, IL: University of Chicago Press.

Farrington, D. P. (1995). The development of offending and antisocial behavior from childhood: Key findings from the Cambridge study in delinquent development. *Journal of Child Psychology and Psychiatry, 36*, 929–964.

Farrington, D. P., Ohlin, L. E., & Wilson, J. Q. (1986). *Understanding and controlling crime: Toward a new research strategy*. New York, NY: Springer-Verlag.

Forrester, D. H., Chatterton, M. R., & Pease, K. (1988). *The Kirkholt burglary prevention project, Rochdale*. London: Home Office (Crime Prevention Paper No. 13).

Fox, R. G., & Freiberg, A. (1985). *Sentencing: State and Federal Law in Victoria*. Melbourne: Oxford University Press.

Frost, N. A., Phillips, N. D., & Clear, T. R. (2007). Productivity of criminal justice scholars across the career. *Journal of Criminal Justice Education, 18*, 428–443.

Garfield, E. (1979). Is citation analysis a legitimate evaluation tool? *Scientometrics, 1*, 359–375.

Garland, D. (1990). *Punishment and modern society*. Oxford: Clarendon Press.

Garland, D. (2001). *The culture of control*. Oxford: Oxford University Press.

Gordon, R. A., & Vicari, P. J. (1992). Eminence in social psychology: A comparison of textbook citation, Social Sciences Citation Index, and research productivity ratings. *Personality and Social Psychology Bulletin, 18*, 26–38.

Gottfredson, M. R., & Hirschi, T. (1986). The true value of lambda would appear to be zero. *Criminology, 24*, 213–234.

Gottfredson, M. R., & Hirschi, T. (1990). *A general theory of crime*. Stanford, CA: Stanford University Press.

Hagan, J. (1974). Extra-legal attributes and criminal sentencing: An assessment of a sociological viewpoint. *Law & Society Review, 8*, 357–384.

Hamilton, D. P. (1990). Publishing by—and for?—the numbers. *Science, 250*, 1331–1332.

Hamilton, D. P. (1991). Research papers: Who's uncited now? *Science, 251*, 25.

Hanson, R. K., & Bussière, M. T. (1998). Predicting relapse: A meta-analysis of sexual offender recidivism studies. *Journal of Consulting and Clinical Psychology, 61,* 646–652.
Hanson, R. K., & Morton-Bourgon, K. E. (2005). The characteristics of persistent sexual offenders: A meta-analysis of recidivism studies. *Journal of Consulting and Clinical Psychology, 73,* 1154–1163.
Hare, R. D. (2003). *The Psychopathy Checklist—revised* (2nd ed.). Toronto, ON: Multi-Health Systems.
Hindelang, M. J., Hirschi, T., & Weis, J. G. (1981). *Measuring delinquency.* Beverly Hills, CA: Sage.
Hirschi, T. (1969). *Causes of delinquency.* Berkeley, CA: University of California Press.
Hough, J. M., & Mayhew, P. M. (1983). *British Crime Survey: First report.* London: Her Majesty's Stationary Office.
Jascó, P. (2008a). Savvy searching: Google Scholar revisited. *Online Information Review, 30,* 102–114.
Jascó, P. (2008b). The pros and cons of computing the h-index using Google Scholar. *Online Information Review, 32,* 437–452.
Jascó, P. (2009a). Google Scholar's ghost authors. *Library Journal, 134,* 26–27.
Jascó, P. (2009b). A final joy write: Panorama of past pans. *Online: Exploring Technology and Resources for Information Professionals, 33,* 51–53.
Jennings, W. G., Gibson, C. L., Ward, J. T., & Beaver, K. M. (2008). "Which group are you in?": A preliminary investigation of group-based publication trajectories of criminology and criminal justice scholars. *Journal of Criminal Justice Education, 19,* 227–250.
Jennings, W. G., Schreck, C. J., Sturtz, M., & Mahoney, M. (2008). Exploring the scholarly output of academic organization leadership in criminology and criminal justice: A research note on publication productivity. *Journal of Criminal Justice Education, 19,* 404–416.
Johnston, L., & Shearing, C. D. (2003). *Governing security.* New York, NY: Routledge.
Khey, D. N., Jennings, W. G., Higgins, G. E., Schoepfer, A., & Langton, L. (2011). Re-ranking the top female academic 'stars' in criminology and criminal justice using an alternate method: A research note. *Journal of Criminal Justice Education, 22,* 118–129.
Kleck, G., & Barnes, J. C. (2011). Article productivity among the faculty of criminology and criminal justice doctoral programs, 2005–2009. *Journal of Criminal Justice Education, 22,* 43–66.
Kleck, G., Wang, S. K., & Tark, J. (2007). Article productivity among the faculty of criminology and criminal justice doctoral programs, 2000–2005. *Journal of Criminal Justice Education, 18,* 385–405.
Laband, D. N., & Piette, M. J. (1994). A citation analysis of the impact of blinded peer review. *Journal of the American Medical Association, 272,* 147–149.
Land, K. C., McCall, P. L., & Nagin, D. S. (1996). A comparison of Poisson, negative binomial, and semiparametric mixed Poisson regression models: With empirical applications to criminal careers research. *Sociological Methods & Research, 24,* 387–442.
Laub, J. H. (2004). The life course of criminology in the United State: The American Society of Criminology 2003 Presidential address. *Criminology, 42,* 1–26.
Laub, J. H., Nagin, D. S., & Sampson, R. J. (1998). Trajectories of change in criminal offending: Good marriages and the desistance process. *American Sociological Review, 63,* 225–238.
Laub, J. H., & Sampson, R. J. (2003). *Shared beginnings, divergent lives.* Cambridge, MA: Harvard University Press.
Lenton, R. L. (1995). Power versus feminist theories of wife abuse. *Canadian Journal of Criminology, 38,* 305–330.
Long, H., Boggess, L. N., & Jennings, W. G. (2011). Re-assessing publication productivity among academic 'stars' in criminology and criminal justice. *Journal of Criminal Justice Education, 22,* 102–117.
Lotz, R., & Regoli, R. M. (1977). Police cynicism and professionalism. *Human Relations, 30,* 175–186.
Lynam, D. R., Caspi, A., Moffitt, T., Wikstrom, P., Loeber, R., & Novak, S. (2000). The interaction between impulsivity and neighborhood context on offending: The effects of impulsivity are stronger in poorer neighborhoods. *Journal of Abnormal Psychology, 109,* 563–574.

References

Marshall, W. L., & Barbaree, H. E. (1988). The long-term evaluation of a behavioral treatment program for child molesters. *Behavior Research and Therapy, 26*, 499–511.

Mayhew, P. M., Elliott, D., & Dowds, L. (1989). *The 1988 British Crime Survey* (Home Office Research Study no. 111.). London: Her Majesty's Stationary Office.

Meadows, A. J. (1974). *Communication in science.* London: Butterworths.

Megargee, E. I., & Bohn, M. J. (1979). *Classifying criminal offenders: A new system based on the MMPI.* Beverly Hills, CA: Sage.

Meho, L. I., & Yang, K. (2007). Impact of data sources on citation counts and rankings of LIS faculty: Web of Science versus Scopus and Google Scholar. *Journal of the American Society for Information Science and Technology, 58*, 2105–2125.

Moffitt, T. E. (1993). Adolescence-limited and life-course-persistent antisocial behavior: A developmental taxonomy. *Psychological Review, 100*, 674–701.

Moffitt, T. E., Caspi, A., Rutter, M., & Silva, P. A. (2001). *Sex differences in antisocial behaviour.* Cambridge: Cambridge University Press.

Myers, C. R. (1970). Journal citations and scientific eminence in contemporary psychology. *American Psychologist, 25*, 1041–1048.

Nagin, D. S. (1999). Analyzing developmental trajectories: A semi-parametric group based approach. *Psychological Methods, 4*, 139–157.

Nagin, D. S. (2005). *Group-based modeling of development.* Cambridge, MA: Harvard University Press.

Nagin, D. S., & Farrington, D. P. (1992). The stability of criminal potential from childhood to adulthood. *Criminology, 30*, 235–260.

Nagin, D. S., Farrington, D. P., & Moffitt, T. E. (1995). Life-course trajectories of different types of offenders. *Criminology, 33*, 111–139.

Nagin, D. S., & Land, K. C. (1993). Age, criminal careers, and population heterogeneity: Specification and estimation of a nonparametric, mixed Poisson model. *Criminology, 31*, 327–362.

Oliver, W. M., Swindell, S., Marks, J., & Balusek, K. (2009). Book 'em Dano': The scholarly productivity of institutions and their faculty in criminal justice books. *Southwest Journal of Criminal Justice, 6*, 59–78.

Orrick, E. A., & Weir, H. (2011). The most prolific sole and lead authors in elite criminology and criminal justice journals, 2000–2009. *Journal of Criminal Justice Education, 22*, 24–42.

Parker, L. C., & Goldfeder, E. (1979). Productivity ratings of graduate programs in criminal justice based on publication in ten critical journals. *Journal of Criminal Justice, 7*, 125–133.

Paternoster, R., Brame, R., Mazerolle, P., & Piquero, A. R. (1998). Using the correct statistical test for the equality of regression coefficients. *Criminology, 36*, 859–866.

Peritz, B. C. (1983). Are methodological papers more cited than theoretical or empirical ones? The case of sociology. *Scientometrics, 5*, 211–218.

Peterson, R. D., & Hagan, J. H. (1984). Changing conceptions of race: Towards an account of anomalous findings of sentencing research. *American Sociological Review, 49*, 56–70.

Piquero, A. R., Farrington, D. P., & Blumstein, A. (2003). The criminal career paradigm. In M. Tonry (Ed.), *Crime and justice* (Vol. 30, pp. 359–506). Chicago, IL: University of Chicago Press.

Piquero, A. R., Farrington, D. P., & Blumstein, A. (2007). *Key issues in criminal career research.* Cambridge: Cambridge University Press.

Piquero, A. R., Jennings, W. G., & Farrington, D. P. (2010). On the malleability of self-control: theoretical and policy implications regard a general theory of crime. *Justice Quarterly, 27*, 803–834.

Poole, E. D., & Regoli, R. M. (1981). Periodical prestige in criminology and criminal justice: A comment. *Criminology, 19*, 470–478.

Pratt, T. C., & Cullen, F. T. (2000). The empirical status of Gottfredson and Hirschi's general theory of crime: A meta-analysis. *Criminology, 38*, 931–964.

Pratt, T. C., & Cullen, F. T. (2005). Assessing macro-level predictors and theories of crime: A meta-analysis. In M. Tonry (Ed.), *Crime and justice* (Vol. 32, pp. 373–450). Chicago, IL: University of Chicago Press.

Raudenbush, S. W., & Bryk, A. S. (2002). *Hierarchical linear models*. Thousand Oaks, CA: Sage (Multiple editions).

Regoli, R. M., Poole, E. D., & Miracle, A. W. (1982). Assessing the prestige of journals in criminal justice: A research note. *Journal of Criminal Justice, 10*, 57–67.

Reiss, A. J., & Farrington, D. P. (1991). Advancing knowledge about co-offending: Results from a prospective longitudinal survey of London males. *Journal of Criminal Law and Criminology, 82*, 360–395.

Rice, S. K., Cohn, E. G., & Farrington, D. P. (2005). Where are they now? Trajectories of publication 'stars' from American criminology and criminal justice programs. *Journal of Criminal Justice Education, 16*, 244–264.

Rice, S. K., Terry, K. J., Miller, H. V., & Ackerman, A. R. (2007). Research trajectories of female scholars in criminology and criminal justice. *Journal of Criminal Justice Education, 18*, 360–384.

Roberts, J. V. (1992). Public opinion, crime, and criminal justice. In M. Tonry (Ed.), *Crime and justice* ((pp, Vol. 16, pp. 99–180). Chicago, IL: University of Chicago Press.

Roberts, J. V. (2002). *The use of victim impact statements in sentencing: A review of international research findings*. Ottawa: Policy Centre for Victim Issues, Department of Justice Canada.

Roberts, J. V., & Gabor, T. (2004). Living in the shadow of prison: Lessons from the Canadian experience in decarceration. *British Journal of Criminology, 44*, 92–112.

Roberts, J. V., & Hough, J. M. (2005). *Understanding public attitudes to criminal justice*. Maidenhead: Open University Press.

Roberts, J. V., & LaPrairie, C. (2000). *Rapport de recherché concernant la condemnation à l'emprisonnement avec sursis au Canada*. Rapport préparé pour le ministère de la Justice du Canada.

Roberts, J. V., & Melchers, R. (2003). The incarceration of Aboriginal offenders: Trends from 1978 to 2001. *Canadian Journal of Criminology and Criminal Justice, 45*, 211–243.

Roberts, J. V., & Stalans, L. J. (1997). *Public opinion, crime, and criminal justice*. Boulder, CO: Westview Press.

Roberts, J. V., Stalans, L. J., Indermaur, D., & Hough, J. M. (2003). *Penal populism and public opinion*. New York: Oxford University Press.

Rushton, J. P., & Endler, N. S. (1979). More to-do about citation counts in British psychology. *Bulletin of the British Psychological Society, 32*, 107–109.

Sampson, R. J., & Laub, J. H. (1993). *Crime in the making: Pathways and turning points through life*. Cambridge, MA: Harvard University Press.

Sampson, R. J., Raudenbush, S. W., & Earls, F. (1997). Neighborhoods and violent crime: A multilevel study of collective efficacy. *Science, 277*, 918–924.

Scopus. (2013). *SciVerse Scopus content coverage guide*. Retrieved April 24, 2013, from http://files.sciverse.com/documents/pdf/ContentCoverageGuide-jan-2013.pdf

Sherman, L. W. (1992). *Policing domestic violence: Experiments and dilemmas*. New York, NY: Free Press.

Sherman, L. W., Gartin, P. R., & Buerger, M. E. (1989). Hot spots of predatory crime: Routine activities and the criminology of place. *Criminology, 27*, 27–55.

Sherman, L. W., Gottfredson, D., MacKenzie, D., Eck, J., Reuter, P., & Bushway, S. (1997). *Preventing crime: What works, what doesn't, what's promising*. Washington, DC: Department of Justice, Office of Justice Programs.

Shichor, D., O'Brien, R. M., & Decker, D. L. (1981). Prestige of journals in criminology and criminal justice. *Criminology, 19*, 461–469.

Shutt, J. E., & Barnes, J. C. (2008). Reexamining criminal justice 'star power' in a larger sky: A belated response to Rice et al. on sociological influence in criminology and criminal justice. *Journal of Criminal Justice Education, 19*, 213–226.

Sorensen, J. R. (2009). An assessment of the relative impact of criminal justice and criminology journals. *Journal of Criminal Justice, 37*, 505–511.

Sorenson, J. R. (1994). Scholarly productivity in criminal justice: Institutional affiliation of authors in the top ten criminal justice journals. *Journal of Criminal Justice, 22*, 535–547.

References

Sorenson, J. R., Patterson, A. L., & Widmayer, A. (1992). Publication productivity of faculty members in criminology and criminal justice doctoral programs. *Journal of Criminal Justice Education, 3*, 1–33.

Sorenson, J. R., Patterson, A. L., & Widmayer, A. (1993). Measuring faculty productivity in a multidisciplinary field: A response to Professor Marenin. *Journal of Criminal Justice Education, 4*, 193–196.

Sorenson, J. R., & Pilgrim, R. (2002). The institutional affiliations of authors in leading criminology and criminal justice journals. *Journal of Criminal Justice, 30*, 11–18.

Stack, S. (1987). Measuring the relative impacts of criminology and criminal justice journals: A research note. *Justice Quarterly, 4*, 475–484.

Stack, S. (2001). The effect of field of terminal degree on scholarly productivity: An analysis of criminal justice faculty. *Journal of Criminal Justice Education, 12*, 19–34.

Steffensmeier, D. J., & Demuth, S. (2000). Ethnicity and sentencing outcomes in U.S. federal courts: Who is punished more harshly? *American Sociological Review, 65*(705), 729.

Steffensmeier, D. J., Ulmer, J. T., & Kramer, J. (1998). The interaction of race, gender, and age in criminal sentencing: The punishment cost of being young, black, and male. *Criminology, 36*, 763–798.

Steiner, B., & Schwartz, J. (2006). The scholarly productivity of institutions and their faculty in leading criminology and criminal justice journals. *Journal of Criminal Justice, 34*, 393–400.

Steiner, B., & Schwartz, J. (2007). Assessing the quality of doctoral programs in criminology in the United States. *Journal of Criminal Justice Education, 18*, 53–86.

Stenning, P., & Roberts, J. V. (2001). Empty promises: Parliament, the Supreme Court, and the sentencing of aboriginal offenders. *Saskatchewan Law Review, 64*, 137–168.

Straus, M. A., Gelles, R. J., & Steinmetz, S. K. (1980). *Behind closed doors: Violence in the American family*. New York, NY: Doubleday.

Taggart, W. A., & Holmes, M. D. (1991). Institutional productivity in criminal justice and criminology: An examination of author affiliation in selected journals. *Journal of Criminal Justice, 19*, 549–561.

Thomas, C. W., & Bronick, M. J. (1984). The quality of doctoral programs in deviance, criminology, and criminal justice: An empirical assessment. *Journal of Criminal Justice, 12*, 21–37.

Thomson Reuters. (2013). *Journal coverage changes*. Retrieved April 24, 2013, from http://ip-science.thomsonreuters.com/cgi-bin/jrnlst/jlcovchanges.cgi?PC=MASTER

Vaughn, M. S., Del Carmen, R. V., Perfecto, M., & Charand, K. X. (2004). Journals in criminal justice and criminology: An updated and expanded guide for authors. *Journal of Criminal Justice Education, 15*, 61–192.

West, D. J., & Farrington, D. P. (1977). *The delinquent way of life*. London: Heinemann.

Wilson, J. Q., & Herrnstein, R. J. (1985). *Crime and human nature*. New York, NY: Simon & Schuster.

Wolfgang, M. E., Figlio, R. M., & Sellin, T. (1972). *Delinquency in a birth cohort*. Chicago, IL: University of Chicago Press.

Wolfgang, M. E., Figlio, R. M., & Thornberry, T. P. (1978). *Evaluating criminology*. New York, NY: Elsevier.

Wright, R. A., & Cohn, E. G. (1996). The most-cited scholars in criminal justice textbooks, 1989 to 1993. *Journal of Criminal Justice, 24*, 459–467.

About the Authors

Ellen G. Cohn is Associate Professor of Criminal Justice and an affiliated faculty member in Women's Studies at Florida International University. Her research focuses primarily on the effect of weather, spatial, and temporal variables on crime and criminal behavior and she is currently collaborating on an international research program that is examining the impact of these factors in a global environment.

David P. Farrington, O.B.E., is Emeritus Professor of Psychological Criminology and Leverhulme Trust Emeritus Fellow at the Institute of Criminology, Cambridge University. His major research interest is in developmental criminology, and he is Director of the Cambridge Study in Delinquent Development, which is a prospective longitudinal survey of over 400 London males from age 8 to age 56. In addition to over 590 published journal articles and book chapters on criminological and psychological topics, he has published 93 books, monographs, and government publications.

Amaia Iratzoqui is a doctoral student in the College of Criminology and Criminal Justice at Florida State University. She holds a Bachelors degree in Criminal Justice and a Masters degree in Public administration from Florida International University. Her current research focusses on gender and rehabilitation programming and victimization as an ongoing risk factor for offending.

Name Index

A
Ackerman, A.R., 3
Ageton, S.S., 8
Agnew, R., 36, 48, 49, 52–55, 57, 58, 62, 64, 65, 79
Akers, R.L., 36, 49, 54, 55, 57, 62, 66, 78
Albonetti, C., 37, 55
Alpert, G.P., 58
Anderson, E., 37, 56
Andrews, D.A., 11, 33, 34, 59–61, 63, 64, 66, 76–78, 90
Applegate, B.K., 81
Arthur, M.W., 29

B
Bakkalbasi, N., 16
Bala, N., 33, 34
Balusek, K., 3
Barbaree, H.E., 59
Barnes, J.C., 3, 21
Barr, R., 6, 7
Bauer, K., 16
Bauman, Z., 31, 34
Baumer, E.P., 56
Bayley, D.H., 31, 42, 58
Beaver, K.M., 3
Beck, U., 31, 34, 39
Bigo, D., 72
Blair, R.J., 61, 72
Blumstein, A., 4–11, 29, 34, 36, 39, 41, 46, 47, 49, 51, 53, 55, 57, 58, 65, 67, 68, 76–81, 87
Boggess, L.N., 3
Bohn, M.J., 59

Bonta, J.L., 10, 11, 33, 34, 59, 60, 63, 66, 72, 74, 76–80, 90
Bottoms, A.E., 29, 31
Bourdieu, P., 31, 34
Bowling, B., 31
Braithwaite, J., 5–7, 10, 28–31, 38, 39, 73, 75, 77, 79, 89
Brame, R., 9, 29, 36, 40, 46, 47, 49, 51, 53, 55, 58, 65, 79, 81, 90
Brantingham, P.J., 16, 22, 30, 46
Brantingham, P.L., 16, 22, 30, 46
Broadhurst, R.G., 29
Brochu, S., 72
Bronick, M.J., 2
Bryk, A.S., 37, 82, 90
Buerger, M.E., 54
Bursik, R.J., 36, 46, 48, 49, 51, 54, 55, 57, 58, 62, 64, 65, 77, 79
Bushway, S.D., 36, 37, 46, 47, 52, 53, 66
Bussière, M.T., 82, 90

C
Caetano, R., 72
Campbell, J.C., 72
Cantor, D., 48
Carrington, P.J., 34
Caspi, A., 36, 41, 47–49, 51, 58, 60, 65, 78, 81
Catalano, R.F., 29
Cesaroni, C., 34
Chan, J.B.L., 28, 29
Chapman, A.J., 13
Charand, K.X., 17
Chatterton, M.R., 30
Chiricos, T.G., 37, 54

Clarke, R.V., 10, 29, 31, 36, 38, 39, 50, 88, 89
Clear, T.R., 3, 6, 10, 44, 61, 80, 88–90
Cohen, J., 15, 16, 22, 23, 29, 34, 46, 47, 50, 52, 66, 67
Cohen, L.E., 7–9, 36, 46, 49, 51, 66, 75
Cohen, S., 4, 6, 28, 30–32, 34, 38, 40, 78
Cohn, E.G., 1–13, 15–21, 23, 25, 43, 67, 73, 87–89, 92
Cole, J., 12
Cole, S., 12, 13
Cormier, C.A., 59, 60
Cornish, D.B., 10, 89
Covington, S., 72
Cullen, F.T., 3, 8–11, 29, 31, 34, 36–39, 41, 46, 49, 51, 54–62, 64, 65, 67, 68, 71–84, 87–89
Cunneen, C., 28, 29, 72

D
Daly, K., 28, 29
Davis, A., 3, 72
Davis, J., 3
Decker, D.L., 18
Decker, S.H., 55, 57, 63, 66
DeKeseredy, W.S., 72
Del Carmen, R.V., 17
Demuth, S., 82
Dess, H.M., 16
DeZee, M.R., 2, 3
Dishion, T.J., 89
Dodge, K.A., 60
Doob, A.N., 33, 34, 38, 40
Douglas, K.S., 61
Douglas, R.J., 13
Dowds, L., 30
Durkheim, E., 31

E
Earls, F.J., 2, 37, 41, 50, 80–82, 89
Eck, J.E., 46
Edens, J.F., 60
Elliott, D.S., 8, 9, 36, 37, 46–49, 52, 53, 66
Endler, N.S., 12
Engel, R.S., 57
Ericson, R.V., 5–7, 31, 33, 34, 39, 72, 74, 75, 78
Esbensen, F.-A., 55

F
Fabianic, D.A., 3, 18
Fagan, J.A., 55
Farrall, S., 31, 32

Farrington, D.P., 1–13, 15–21, 23, 25, 28, 29, 31, 32, 34, 36, 38, 39, 41–43, 46, 47, 49–51, 53, 55, 57, 59–62, 64, 65, 67, 68, 71–84, 87–89, 92
Feeley, M.M., 31
Felson, M., 8, 9, 29, 36, 46, 49, 51, 66
Felson, R.B., 56
Figlio, R.M., 2, 6, 47
Finkelhor, D., 72, 73
Fisher, B.S., 56, 57, 81
Forrester, D.H., 30
Forth, A.E., 60
Foshee, V.A., 72
Foucault, M., 31–34, 39, 72–74, 76, 78–80
Fox, R.G., 28
Frank, J., 9, 56, 58
Freiberg, A., 28, 29
Frick, P.J., 59, 60
Frost, N.A., 3

G
Gabor, T., 33
Garfield, E., 13
Garland, D., 5–7, 28–31, 34, 38, 39, 41, 43, 72–74, 76, 78–80
Gartin, P.R., 54
Gelles, R.J., 10, 33, 77
Gendreau, P., 33, 34, 58, 60, 72, 78
Gibson, C.L., 3
Giddens, A., 30, 31
Gilbert, K.E., 10, 54, 88
Giordano, P.C., 50
Goffman, E., 32
Goggin, C.E., 60
Goldfeder, E., 3, 18
Goldkamp, J.S., 72
Gordon, R.A., 12
Gottfredson, D.C., 6, 7, 28
Gottfredson, M.R., 5–11, 29, 33, 35, 36, 38, 39, 46–49, 51, 53, 55, 57, 60–62, 64, 65, 67, 73, 74, 78, 79, 89, 90
Grasmick, H.G., 8, 36, 46, 49, 51, 54, 55, 57, 62, 65, 75, 77, 79
Grisso, T., 60
Gudjonsson, G., 72
Gusterson, H., 72

H
Hagan, J.L., 8, 36, 49, 54–58, 62, 64, 65
Haggerty, K.D., 6, 7, 33, 34
Hall, S., 32
Hall, W., 30

Name Index

Hamilton, D.P., 71
Hannah-Moffat, K., 33, 34
Hanson, R.K., 34, 59, 60, 63, 72–74, 76, 78–80, 82, 83, 90
Hare, R.D., 34, 59, 60, 63, 66, 72–75, 78
Harris, G.T., 60, 74, 76, 78
Hart, S.D., 60
Hartnagel, T.J., 34
Hawkins, J.D., 29
Haynie, D.L., 48, 49
Herrnstein, R.J., 6
Higgins, G.E., 3
Hindelang, M.J., 7, 9, 49, 67, 79
Hirschi, T., 5–11, 22, 29, 33, 35–39, 42, 46–51, 53–57, 60–62, 64, 65, 67, 68, 72–75, 78–80, 87–90
Hoge, R.D., 60
Holmes, M.D., 3
Homel, R.J., 28
Horwood, L.J., 30
Hough, J.M., 29–32, 34, 39, 42
Hudson, B., 30, 31
Huizinga, D., 8, 29, 37, 49, 53, 55, 66

I
Indermauer, D., 29, 72

J
Jacobs, B.A., 15, 22, 31
Jascó, P., 16
Jefferson, T., 31, 72
Jennings, W.G., 3, 89
Johnston, L., 98

K
Kelling, G.L., 72
Kennedy, R.B., 34
Khey, D.N., 3
Kleck, G., 3
Knight, K., 61
Koss, M.P., 72–74, 78, 80
Kramer, J.H., 36, 37, 55, 72, 74, 75, 77, 78, 82
Krohn, M.D., 37, 49, 53, 55, 57, 63, 66

L
Laband, D.N., 71
Land, K.C., 36, 46, 47, 49, 51, 53, 56, 65
Landry, M., 72
Langton, L., 3
LaPrairie, C., 33, 35
Latessa, E.J., 60

Laub, J.H., 2, 6–11, 22, 28, 29, 31, 34–36, 38, 39, 41, 43, 45–51, 53–55, 57, 61, 62, 65, 68, 71, 72, 74–90
Lauritsen, J.L., 36, 49, 54, 55, 66
Lenton, R.L., 33
Leo, R.A., 72
Levenson, J.S., 74, 75
Levi, M., 31, 75
Levitt, S.D., 46
Lillienfeld, S.O., 61
Lind, B., 29
Lind, E.A., 72
Link, B.G., 9, 56
Liska, A.E., 36, 50
Lizotte, A.J., 56
Loader, I., 31, 32, 72
Loeber, R., 8, 23, 29, 34, 37, 40, 46, 49, 51, 55, 57, 60, 62, 65, 72, 77–79
Long, H., 3
Lotz, R., 58
Lynam, D.R., 60, 64

M
MacKenzie, D.L., 58
Maguire, E.R., 72
Mahoney, M., 3
Marks, J., 3
Marshall, W.L., 59, 60, 72
Maruna, S., 31
Mastrofski, S.D., 55
Matthews, R.A., 72
Maxwell, G., 29
Mayhew, P.M., 30
Mazerolle, P.J., 9, 37, 49, 53, 55, 57, 58, 62, 64, 66, 81, 90
McCall, P.L., 47
McCord, J., 89
McEvoy, K., 32
Meadows, A.J., 2
Meehl, P.E., 60
Megargee, E.I., 59
Meho, L.I., 16
Melchers, R., 33
Messner, S.F., 36, 46, 50, 51, 55, 57, 62, 65, 67, 73
Miethe, T.D., 47, 49, 57, 66
Miller, H.V., 3
Miller, J., 30
Miracle, A.W., 18
Mitchell, K.J., 72
Moffitt, T.E., 5, 7, 8, 10, 11, 28, 29, 33–36, 38, 39, 41, 46–51, 55–57, 59–62, 64, 65, 67, 68, 72–74, 76, 78–82, 87, 89, 90
Monahan, J.T., 59, 60

Morenoff, J.D., 36, 37, 46, 50, 52, 66, 73, 78
Morris, A., 29
Morton-Gourgon, K.E., 61, 82, 90
Mullins, C.W., 72
Mulvey, E.P., 60
Myers, C.R., 12

N
Nagin, D.S., 6, 7, 9, 28, 29, 31, 36, 38, 39, 41, 43, 46, 47, 49–51, 53, 54, 57, 61, 64, 65, 67, 68, 71–74, 76–79, 81, 82, 87, 90
Newburn, T., 30, 31
Novak, S., 99

O
O'Brien, R.M., 18
O'Leary, K.D., 72–74, 78
O'Malley, P., 5, 22, 31, 32, 34, 39, 42
O'Malley, P.M., 42
Ohlin, L.E., 11, 89
Oliver, W.M., 3
Orrick, E.A., 3
Osgood, D.W., 36, 46, 48, 49, 51, 53, 65, 67, 72

P
Parazelli, M., 72
Parker, H., 32
Parker, L.C., 3, 18
Paternoster, R., 8, 9, 28, 29, 36, 39, 46, 49–51, 53, 55, 57, 61, 62, 65, 68, 71, 72, 74, 76, 78, 79, 81, 90
Patterson, A.L., 2
Pavlich, G., 34
Pease, K., 5–7, 29, 30, 32, 47
Perfecto, M., 17
Peritz, B.C., 13
Petersilia, J., 58, 73, 77
Peterson, R.D., 37, 54
Phillips, C., 32
Phillips, N.D., 3
Piehl, A.M., 47
Piette, M.J., 71
Pilgrim, R., 3
Piquero, A.R., 9, 11, 23, 28, 29, 32, 34, 36, 38, 39, 41, 46–51, 53–62, 64, 65, 67, 68, 71–83, 89, 90
Poole, E.D., 18
Poulin, F., 89
Pratt, J., 29
Pratt, T.C., 9, 37, 41, 48, 49, 55–58, 60–62, 64, 65, 67, 80, 81

Prendergast, M.L., 72
Price, D.H., 72

Q
Quinsey, V.L., 35, 60

R
Raine, A., 60
Raudenbush, S.W., 2, 29, 36, 37, 40, 41, 46, 47, 49–51, 55, 57, 62, 65, 71–74, 76–84, 89, 90
Regoli, R.M., 18, 58
Reiner, R., 31, 72
Reisig, M.D., 57
Reiss, A.J., 89
Reuter, P., 3, 15
Rice, M.E., 59, 60, 74, 76, 78
Rice, S.K., 3, 21
Roberts, J.V., 29, 31, 33, 34, 39, 42, 43
Rogers, R., 60
Rokeach, M., 72
Rose, N.S., 31, 32, 34, 38, 39
Rosenbaum, P.R., 46
Rosenfeld, R., 36, 45, 52, 56, 58, 66
Roth, J.A., 6
Roth, L.H., 59
Rubin, D.B., 46
Rushton, J.P., 12
Rutter, M., 81

S
Sampson, R.J., 2, 5–11, 22, 23, 28, 29, 31, 33–36, 38, 39, 41–43, 45–51, 53–57, 60–62, 64, 65, 67, 68, 71–85, 87, 89, 90
Schoepfer, A., 3
Schreck, C.J., 3, 50
Schulenberg, J.L., 34
Schwartz, J., 3, 21
Schwartz, M.D., 72
Schwartz, S.-H., 72
Sellin, T., 6, 47
Shaw, M., 34
Shearing, C.D., 29, 31, 32, 34, 39, 42, 72, 77
Sherman, L.W., 5–8, 10, 11, 28–31, 33, 36, 40, 46, 54, 55, 57, 58, 62, 64, 65, 68, 73, 75, 77, 79, 89, 90
Shichor, D., 18
Shutt, J.E., 3, 21
Silva, P.A., 41, 49, 81
Simon, J., 31, 32
Simpson, D.D., 59, 60

Skogan, W.G., 8, 32, 56–58, 64, 67, 72, 78–80
Smith, D., 16, 22
Smith, D.A., 8, 56, 72
Sorenson, J.R., 2, 3
Spade, D., 72
Sparks, J.R., 22, 31
Spohn, C.C., 35, 36, 47, 54, 55, 57, 61, 63, 66, 67, 72, 74, 76, 78, 79
Stack, S., 3, 18
Stalans, L.J., 42
Steadman, H.J., 61
Steffensmeier, D.J., 29, 36, 39, 46, 49, 51, 55, 57, 58, 62, 64, 65, 72, 74, 76–80, 82, 83, 90
Steinberg, L., 61
Steiner, B., 3, 21
Steinmetz, S.K., 33
Stenning, P.C., 33, 34
Stouthamer-Loeber, M., 50, 60
Strang, H., 28
Straus, M.A., 33, 71–78, 80
Sturtz, M., 3
Swindell, S., 3

T

Taggart, W.A., 3
Tark, J., 3
Taylor, R.B., 35, 36, 46, 48, 55, 56
Terry, K.J., 3
Testa, M., 72
Tewksbury, R., 54, 55, 72, 75, 78
Thomas, C.W., 2
Thornberry, T.P., 2
Thornton, D., 60
Tittle, C.R., 36, 48, 55, 57, 66
Toch, H., 61
Tombs, S., 31
Tonry, M.H., 20, 41, 47, 81
Tremblay, R.E., 29, 46
Tuch, S.A., 58
Tyler, T.R., 29, 31, 32, 34, 38, 39, 54, 55, 57, 58, 62, 66, 72, 74–79

U

Ulmer, J.T., 36, 46, 72, 74, 78, 82
Umbreit, M.S., 35

V

Vaughn, M.S., 35
Vicari, P.J., 12
Visher, C.A., 6, 56
Vitaro, F., 72

W

Wacquant, L., 31
Walker, S., 58
Walters, G.D., 60
Wang, S.K., 3
Ward, J.T., 3
Ward, T., 60, 72
Warr, M., 32, 35, 36, 46, 49, 52, 53, 56, 57, 66
Weatherburn, D., 28, 29
Webster, C.D., 59
Weir, H., 3
Weis, J.G., 9
Weisburd, D.L., 37, 46, 47, 55, 66, 72, 73, 78–80
Weitzer, R., 54, 55, 57, 62, 66
West, D.J., 6
Wexler, D.B., 35
Widmayer, A., 2
Wikstrom, P., 30
Wilson, J.Q., 4, 6–8, 11, 58, 89
Wilson, W.J., 36, 55, 67
Wolfe, N.T., 9, 56
Wolfgang, M.E., 2, 4–11, 47, 67, 73, 75, 77, 79
Worden, R.E., 57, 58, 75
Wortley, S., 34
Wright, J.P., 48, 49, 57
Wright, R.A., 2, 16, 19, 22, 88
Wright, R.T., 31, 37

Y

Yang, K., 16
Young, J., 28, 31, 32, 38, 72, 74, 75

Z

Zedner, L., 30, 31
Zhao, J., 72
Zinger, I., 35

Subject Index

A

Academy of Criminal Justice Sciences (ACJS), 19
Adolescence-limited and life-course persistent antisocial behavior (Moffitt), 11, 41, 61, 81, 87, 89
Age and crime (Farrington), 8, 9, 53, 61
Age, criminal careers, and population heterogeneity (Nagin and Land), 47, 53
AHCI. *See* Arts and Humanities Citation Index (AHCI)
American Journal of Drug and Alcohol Abuse, 17
American Society of Criminology (ASC), 17, 20, 27, 87
American Sociological Review, 17, 82
Analyzing developmental trajectories: A semi-parametric group based approach (Nagin), 81
ANZ. *See Australian and New Zealand Journal of Criminology* (ANZ)
Article, defined, 21
Arts and Humanities Citation Index (AHCI), 3
ASC. *See* American Society of Criminology (ASC)
Assessing macro-level predictors and theories of crime: A meta-analysis (Pratt and Cullen), 41
Australian and New Zealand Journal of Criminology (ANZ), 4, 5, 10, 18–20, 27–29, 38–40, 43, 70, 72
Australian and New Zealand Society of Criminology, 18

B

Behavioral Sciences and the Law, 17
Behind Closed Doors (Straus et al.), 33
BJC. *See British Journal of Criminology*
The British Crime Survey (Hough and Mayhew), 30
The 1988 British Crime Survey (Mayhew et al.), 30
British Journal of Criminology (BJC), 4, 10, 17, 19, 20, 27–32, 38–40, 43, 70, 72

C

CAD. *See Crime and Delinquency* (CAD)
CAJ. *See Crime and Justice: A Review of Research* (CAJ)
Canadian Criminal Justice Association, 18
Canadian Journal of Criminology/Canadian Journal of Criminology and Criminal Justice (CJC), 4, 10, 18–20, 27, 32–35, 37, 39, 40, 43, 70
Causes of Delinquency (Hirschi), 8, 11, 35, 47, 48, 53, 61, 88
Changing conceptions of race (Peterson and Hagan), 54
The Characteristics of persistent sexual offenders: A meta-analysis of recidivism studies (Hanson and Morton-Bourgon), 82
Child maltreatment, 17
Citation analysis
 advantages of, 12, 23
 limitations of, 12–13
 policy implications of, 88–90
 reliability, 4, 84

Citation analysis (*cont.*)
 studies (*see* Journals, ranking of)
 validity, 4, 84, 92
Citations
 behavior, 91, 92
 careers, 38, 67, 68, 90
 counting, 3, 4, 12, 21–23, 84
 eligibility, 22
 errors in, 4, 15, 21–23, 88
 sources of, 2–4, 15–17, 24, 25, 42, 83
CJB. *See Criminal Justice and Behavior* (CJB)
CJC. *See Canadian Journal of Criminology/ Canadian Journal of Criminology and Criminal Justice* (CJC)
CJR. *See Criminal Justice Review* (CJR)
Classifying Criminal Offenders (Megargee and Bohn), 59
CLSC. *See Crime, Law, and Social Change* (CLSC)
Coauthor citations, 21, 22, 24, 27, 30, 32, 35, 45, 48, 56, 59, 92
Collective efficacy, research on. 41, 81, 82, 89, 90. *See also* Neighborhoods and violent crime
A Comparison of Poisson, negative binomial, and semiparametric mixed Poisson regression models with empirical applications to criminal careers research (Land et al.), 47
Contemporary Crises. See Crime, Law and Social Change (CLSC)
Corrections Today, 20
CRGE. *See Criminologie* (CRGE)
CRIM. *See Criminology* (CRIM)
Crime and Delinquency (CAD), 7, 10, 18, 70, 72
Crime and Human Nature (Wilson and Herrnstein), 6
Crime and Justice: A Review of Research (CAJ), 19, 20, 70, 72, 73
Crime in the Making (Sampson and Laub), 6–9, 11, 28, 35, 41, 45, 48, 50, 53, 54, 61, 80, 81, 84, 89, 90
Crime, Law, and Social Change (CLSC), 10, 20, 70, 72
Crime placement, displacement, and deflection (Barr and Pease), 6, 7
Crime, Shame, and Reintegration (Braithwaite), 6, 7, 28, 30, 89
Criminal career concepts
 frequency, 12, 23, 90
 prevalence, 12, 23
 specialization, 12, 23, 90
 trajectories, 47, 68, 90
 use of in citation analysis, 2, 12, 23
 versatility, 12, 23, 90
The Criminal career paradigm (Piquero et al.), 11, 41, 53, 61, 80, 81, 90
Criminal career research: Its value for criminology (Blumstein et al.), 6, 10, 11, 41, 81
Criminal Careers and "Career Criminals" (Blumstein et al.), 6, 8, 9, 11
Criminal Justice and Behavior (CJB), 7, 10, 18–21, 45, 58–63, 68, 70, 72, 73
Criminal Justice History, 20
Criminal Justice Review (CJR), 18, 20, 70, 72
Criminologie (CRGE), 10, 20, 70, 72
Criminology (CRIM), 4, 5, 7, 9, 17–19, 22, 27, 35–41, 43, 45, 50–52, 70–73, 81, 82
Criminology and Public Policy, 17, 24, 91
The Culture of Control (Garland), 30, 41, 42

D

Delinquency in a Birth Cohort (Wolfgang et al.), 6, 9, 11, 47
The Delinquent Way of Life (West and Farrington), 6
Development and Psychopathology, 17
The Development of offending and antisocial behavior from childhood (Farrington), 11
Division of International Criminology. 20. *See also* American Society of Criminology (ASC)
Doctoral programs, rankings of. *See* Productivity analysis
Does correctional treatment work? A clinically relevant and psychologically informed meta-analysis (Andrews et al.), 11, 61

E

Elsevier. 3, 16. *See also* Scopus
The Empirical status of Gottfredson and Hirschi's general theory of crime: A meta-analysis (Pratt and Cullen), 9, 41, 56, 61, 80, 81
Empty promises (Stenning and Roberts), 33
Erectile responses among heterosexual child molesters, father-daughter incest offenders and matched nonoffenders (Barbaree and Marshall), 59
Ethnicity and sentencing outcomes in U.S. federal courts: Who is punished more harshly? (Steffensmeier and Demuth), 82

Subject Index

European Journal of Criminology, 17, 24, 43, 91
Evaluating Criminology (Wolfgang et al.), 2
Evaluating Criminology and Criminal Justice (Cohn et al.), 2
Explaining Delinquency and Drug Use (Elliott et al.), 8
Extra-legal attributes and criminal sentencing (Hagan), 56

F
Federal Probation (FP), 10, 18–20, 70, 72, 73
Frequency, 12, 23, 35, 59, 80, 82, 83, 90

G
A General Theory of Crime (Gottfredson and Hirschi), 6–9, 11, 35, 48, 53, 61, 89
Global Options, 20
Google Scholar (GS), 3, 16, 23, 24, 87, 88
Governing Security (Johnson and Shearing), 42
Group-Based Modeling of Development (Nagin), 41, 53, 81
GS. *See* Google Scholar

H
Harvard University, 38, 41, 81
Hierarchical Linear Models (Raudenbush and Bryk), 82
Home Office (UK), 21, 41, 81
Homicide Studies, 17
Hot spots of predatory crime (Sherman et al.), 54
Howard Journal of Criminal Justice, 20

I
IJCA. *See International Journal of Comparative and Applied Criminal Justice* (IJCA)
IJOT. *See International Journal of Offender Therapy and Comparative Criminology* (IJOT)
The Incarceration of Aboriginal offenders (Roberts and Melchers), 33
Influence
    combined measure of, 4, 37, 50, 61, 64
    definition, 2
    scholarly (*see* Scholarly influence)
The Interaction between impulsivity and neighborhood context on offending (Lynam et al.), 64

The Interaction of race, gender, and age in criminal sentencing: The punishment cost of being young, black, and male (Steffensmeier et al.), 82
International Association for Correctional and Forensic Psychology, 20
International Journal of Comparative and Applied Criminal Justice (IJCA), 10, 20, 70, 72, 73
International Journal of Offender Therapy and Comparative Criminology (IJOT), 10, 20, 70, 72, 73

J
JCCJ. *See Journal of Contemporary Criminal Justice* (JCCJ)
JCJ. *See Journal of Criminal Justice* (JCJ)
JCLC. *See Journal of Criminal Law and Criminology* (JCLC)
JIV. *See Journal of Interpersonal Violence* (JIV)
Journal impact factor, 87
Journal of Adolescence, 17
Journal of Crime and Justice, 19, 20
Journal of Criminal Justice (JCJ), 7, 10, 18–20, 23, 45, 56–58, 62, 63, 68, 70, 72
Journal of Criminal Law and Criminology (JCLC), 18, 19
Journal of Experimental Criminology, 17, 24, 91
Journal of Interpersonal Violence (JIV), 10, 20, 70, 72, 73
Journal of Quantitative Criminology (JQC), 7, 9, 18, 19, 45–48, 51, 52, 70–73
Journal of Research in Crime and Delinquency (JRCD), 7, 10, 18, 19, 45, 48–52, 70, 72, 73
Journal of Threat Assessment, 17
Journal of Youth and Adolescence, 17
Journals. *See also* individual journals
    coverage changes, 15
    importance, 1, 84, 85
    parochial nature of, 5, 43
    prestige of, 87, 91
    selection of, 16–18, 91
JQ. *See Justice Quarterly* (JQ)
JQC. *See Journal of Quantitative Criminology* (JQC)
JRCD. *See Journal of Research in Crime and Delinquency* (JRCD)
Justice Quarterly (JQ), 7, 18, 43, 45, 53–56, 70
Juvenile and Family Court Journal, 17

K

Key Issues in Criminal Career Research
(Piquero et al), 41, 81
The Kirkholt Burglary Prevention Project
(Forrester et al.), 30

L

Law and Human Behavior, 17
Law and Social Inquiry, 17
Law and Society Review, 17
Life-course trajectories of different types of offenders (Nagin et al.), 6, 7, 9
Living in the shadow of prison (Roberts and Gabor), 33
The Long-term evaluation of a behavioral treatment program for child molesters (Marshall and Barbaree), 59

M

Measuring Delinquency (Hindelang et al.), 9

N

National Institute of Justice, 21, 42
Nationality of authors, 22
Neighborhoods and violent crime (Sampson et al.), 41, 50, 54, 61, 80–82, 90
The New Structure of Policing
(Bayley and Shearing), 42
New York Times, 21

O

The Onset and persistence of offending (Nagin and Farrington), 6, 7
Oxford University Press, 17, 41, 42

P

Penal Populism and Public Opinion
(Roberts et al.), 42
The Police Chief, 20
Police cynicism and professionalism (Lotz and Regoli), 58
Police Studies, 20
Policing: An International Journal of Police Strategies and Management, 17
Policing Domestic Violence (Sherman), 11, 89
Policing the Risk Society (Ericson and Haggerty), 6, 7
Predicting relapse: A meta-analysis of sexual offender recidivism studies (Hanson and Bussiére), 82

Prevalence, 12, 21, 23, 33, 35, 67, 80, 82–84, 91
Preventing Crime (Sherman et al.), 6, 7, 28, 90
The Prison Journal, 20
Productivity analysis
  studies of, 21
  uses of, 2
The Psychology of Criminal Conduct
(Andrews and Bonta), 11, 59, 90
The Psychopathy Checklist–Revised (Hare), 59
Publication productivity. *See* Productivity analysis
Public opinion about punishment and corrections (Cullen et al.), 81
Public opinion, crime, and criminal justice (Roberts), 33
Public Opinion, Crime, and Criminal Justice
(Roberts & Stalans), 42
Punishment and Modern Society (Garland), 6, 7, 41

R

Rapport de recherché: concernant la condamnation à l' emprisonnement avec sursis au Canada (Roberts and LaPrairie), 33
Reaffirming Rehabilitation (Cullen and Gilbert), 54, 88
The Reasoning Criminal
(Cornish and Clarke), 88

S

Scholarly influence
  measures of, 4, 12, 23, 37, 50, 61, 64, 67, 84, 87
  over time, 5, 7, 25, 83, 85, 87, 88, 91, 92
Scholarly Influence in Criminology and Criminal Justice (Cohn and Farrington), 1, 88
Scholarly productivity. *See* Productivity
Scholars, ranking of
  combined measure of influence, 4, 37, 50, 61, 64
  concordance, 38
Science Citation Index (SCI), 3
Scopus, 3, 16, 23–25, 87
Self-citations, 15, 16, 21, 22, 24, 27, 30, 32, 35, 42, 45, 48, 53, 56, 59, 69, 71, 80, 88, 92
Sentencing (Doob and Roberts), 33
Sentencing (Fox and Freiberg), 28
Sex Differences in Antisocial Behavior
(Moffitt et al.), 41, 81
Shared Beginnings, Divergent Lives
(Laub and Sampson), 41, 81

Subject Index

SJ. *See Social Justice* (SJ)
Social change and crime rate trends:
    A routine activity approach
    (Cohen and Felson), 8
The Social dimensions of correctional officer
    stress (Cullen et al.), 9, 56
Social Forces, 17
Social Justice (SJ), 10, 20, 70–73
Social Problems, 17
Social Sciences Citation Index (SSCI), 3, 15,
    18, 21, 42
Specialization, 12, 23, 35, 43, 82, 83, 90
SSCI. *See* Social Sciences Citation Index (SCI)
The Stability of criminal potential from
    childhood to adulthood
    (Nagin and Farrington), 47
Stockholm Prize in Criminology, 87

T
Thomson Reuters, 3, 15. *See also*
    Web of Science
Trajectories of change in criminal offending,
    (Laub et al.), 47
The True value of lambda would appear to be
    zero (Gottfredson and Hirschi), 11

U
Understanding and Controlling Crime
    (Farrington et al.), 11, 89
Understanding Public Attitudes to Criminal
    Justice (Roberts and Hough), 42
University departments
    citations and, 1
    prestige of, 1
The Use of Victim Impact Statements in
    Sentencing (Roberts), 33
Using the correct statistical test for the
    equality of regression coefficients
    (Paternoster et al.), 9, 53, 61, 81

V
VAV. *See Violence and Victims* (VAV)
Versatility, 12, 23, 28, 30, 33, 35, 42, 43, 45,
    53, 54, 56, 58, 59, 64, 68, 82–84, 90
Victimology, 20
Violence and Victims (VAV), 10, 20, 70
Visions of Social Control (Cohen), 6, 30

W
Web of Science (WoS), 3, 15, 16, 24, 25, 87